# THE
# MIDDLE FORK

*Finding Significance in a Forested Valley*

by
**Brad Allen**

www.middleforkgiants.com

Copyright © 2010 by Brad Allen

Edited by:  Ron Waterman

Cover illustration by:  Ellie Allen

Illustrations by:  the author

Pre-publish comments:  Dave Hunt, Wendy Hunt, Bruce Taber, Mike Davis, Bradley Allen, Ellie Allen


For more information on the big trees and history in
The Middle Fork Valley, please visit:
www.middleforkgiants.com.

www.middleforkgiants.com

Redmond, WA


ISBN 0-7414-5818-7


Printed in the United States of America


Published  January 2010

**INFINITY PUBLISHING**
1094 New DeHaven Street, Suite 100
West Conshohocken, PA 19428-2713
Toll-free (877) BUY BOOK
Local Phone (610) 941-9999
Fax (610) 941-9959
Info@buybooksontheweb.com
www.buybooksontheweb.com

# Preface

In September 2006, while traveling cross-country on a business trip, one of many that year, I spontaneously wrote an essay about my family, kids, and the past few months. That essay explored many of the questions I felt with my kids growing older. I wondered where I would find significance after they left. These thoughts contained hints of the struggles, changes, and the transition I faced. What I didn't foresee is the major part history and an obscure forested valley would play in my life. Reading it now, I can tell I did not have even a clue to the eventual mission I would find.

With that in mind I present:

A Father's Summer

*An essay about the summer of 2006*

Six weeks before sitting on this plane, I sat on a ledge above Lake Kachess while Zach, my youngest son, explored the shoreline below camp. Our two kayaks sat well up on the rocks just to the south. I was reading Edward Abbey's book, Desert Solitaire. An airliner set a pale white contrail across the sky.

I had started Abbey's book the week before while flying on a business trip to Charlotte. The reading was stiff and, at times, forced. I wanted to like the book but somehow it didn't seem to flow. But now, everything had changed in this secluded lakeside campsite.

I could see the lights of another campsite a mile or so down the lake. An earlier exploratory paddle up the lake revealed a second neighbor who, like us, found an isolated site, invisible to the casual observer. Edward Abbey's words were suddenly coming alive: "Alone in a vast wilderness";

the need to protect this wilderness from 'motor-tourism'. How could I arrange to live weeks out here instead of just this isolated Friday night, hemmed in by work, social, and other commitments? Even the bat that flew precariously between my face and the book in search of bugs mesmerized by my headlamp, failed to startle me nor dampen my enthusiasm for the wild.

I really enjoy kayaking with Zach, although I didn't expect to enjoy this little excursion. I loved it. How could we spend more time kayaking together? Another plane set its mark on the evening sky.

I could predict when this summer would end. It would be over at the exact moment when I peered down on this campsite from a plane. Six weeks later my first business trip of the fall ended it. Yet, somehow there was a unique satisfaction in this particular summer.

For me, the distinction of the summer of 2006 is hard to find yet easy to see. My oldest son Bradley just graduated from High School and I am pretty sure our ability to climb together will shortly come to an end. It has been a great run. In the four years since he first summitted Mt. Rainier with me, we have climbed the Grand Teton, the North Face of Mt. Index, Mt. Stuart, The Brothers, repeated Rainier three times, and traversed Half Dome. In some ways our era ended in late June on our fourth Rainier climb.

I started climbing nine years ago with the express goal of climbing Rainier once, and only once. Eighteen months later, with four friends from church, we accomplished that goal, standing on the top of the grand lady of the Northwest. It was the most tiring day of my life. I had lived with a mountain-sized hole inside for years from an unfulfilled goal to climb Mt. Rainier before I was twenty years old. I didn't even attempt it then. Now, fifteen years later, that first summit didn't fill the hole.

Summing with Bradley in 2002 and my daughter Ellie in 2004 seemed to come close to filling the void, but still the mountains called; and The Mountain called. In June of 2006 on a whim, Bradley and I decided to make a one-day car-to-car accent of Rainier. It was a beautiful climb.

At 10:00 PM, as Bradley led over the crater rim, he called back to me about seeing rocks, and he thought we were probably on the rim. Our schedule on this particular climb left us on a moonless night, all alone, as we entered the crater. My laugh-out-loud felt to be a life turning point. What an ironic moment! Seven years before, I had crossed this false crest on the south side of the crater; exhausted, cold, and dazed to the point of bare recollection. Now here I was, having covered the ground since Ingraham Flats in three hours. It took almost eight hours the first time.

I felt great as we lay there in the crater. We dozed and even slept a little, hoping to time our decent to miss the hordes coming up from Camp Muir using a more typical itinerary of summiting just after sunrise. On two occasions volcanic steam, rising slowly from the porous ground on this windless night, startled us. In the starlight the steam took on human shapes and seemed to be approaching. We recalled Dee Molenar's stories in The Challenge of Rainier about mysterious creatures in the crater. With a click of my headlamp, the apparitions disappeared, and we were left alone with the vast midnight crater.

Five weeks later found me on the Wonderland Trail, a 96 mile encirclement of Mt Rainier with 24,000 feet of elevation gain and loss. This trip was scheduled to be a nine-day trip with Ellie, a celebration of the summer before her Junior year. But Ellie was to transition in life more than I during 2006. Instead it became a four-day trip with a friend.

Over Spring break the entire family, including Ann, flew down to Southern Utah for some hiking in the Canyons. Ellie was almost giddy with excitement as we went down into the Grand Gulch of Cedar Mesa. But our time together was tempered with issues she fought in the previous year. Seven years of soccer ended and her relationships at school foundered. She had not detached from us but was in a time of true personal change. Ann and I both felt deeply for her and were working with her through it.

In the Canyons, Ellie came to like the extended time in the wilderness less and less. She obviously felt a burden not to disappoint me but I could see she no longer felt the same way about extended wilderness trips as I did. I assured her it was okay. A month later she made the cheer leading squad, starting a personal recovery and makeover that is, so far, truly remarkable. I do not miss the old Ellie, even though we climbed mountains and backpacked for weeks at a time together. The new Ellie is a remarkable person who I enjoy knowing. To me, she left the ranger station a child and came out of Grand Gulch much more a woman.

The canyons were the start of another change, this one of the Allen family as a whole. In June we went for our annual car drive and camping trip. For the first time in many years a camping vacation did not go well. There were many aspects to this; weather, the locations, family hook ups during the trip, but most of all I think we were all changing. It would surprise me if any of the old recipes for vacations ever work again. So my friend Bruce and I completed the Wonderland trail in four days. I had wanted to hike the full trail since High School.

Ellie and I did go to Mt Rainier. Riding my motorcycle two weeks later we went to Sunrise and had a great time. We reflected over standing on the top two years before. She beamed with pride. A week later I saw her perform at the first Mt. Si Wildcats football game. I was so proud. An old paradigm had passed away. But I wouldn't exchange that summit with my daughter two years before for anything.

I learned last year how each of my kids is unique and how their emotions are very different. Zach didn't want to climb. He just plain spooked big-time on a peak we had gone up just to scramble. He had climbed harder peaks before, the rocks below our kayaking campsite were a tougher climb. He just didn't love the exposure like Bradley did. Zach prepared me for the lesson with Ellie. With kids, it's not about where or what, but only who. Zach is someone unique. He is only twelve.

Bradley led both climbs of Rainier this year. His strength is amazing. He is so even tempered. I wonder about his wilderness judgment. He has only climbed with me and I tend to make the tough calls. He is much more experienced than I was, at eighteen. Then, of course, my judgment seems a bit suspect right now as well.

Immediately following the Wonderland trail hike with Bruce, I set out with Bradley on a cross-country trek through the central Cascade Mountains. A hard first day convinced us to reduce our expectations, camp at an isolated lake, climb a couple of peaks and take a trail out. We would cover only about half of our adventure.

The first mountain, Chikamin Peak, was fun and easy. The next day we headed off to Lemah 3, an isolated, esoteric Northwest destination. Two hours of brutal bushwhacking dropped us onto the glacial moraine where, 35 years earlier, the Lemah Glacier sat when Fred Beckey wrote the route description and took the pictures for his book. Chossy, dirty rockslides led us another mile to the ice. I love ice. The climb was exquisite, not too hard, exposed and with little trace of human use. The descent exposed a mortality I seem, with an adolescent male myopia, to ignore.

The route guide clearly showed a dotted line up a tight gulley leading West of Lemah 1 and to the carved granite valley above our camp. We didn't want to go back through the brush on our way back.

I elected to go first, unroped and alone, in order to avoid knocking rocks down on Bradley. I could see an unstable-looking chockstone halfway up the 500-foot gulley and figured that was the crux. I was wrong. Beyond the chockstone was a cruel world of chest-sized rocks embedded in dirt that looked more like powdered sugar. It quickly went vertical and stones rained down. I couldn't go up or down. I started to shake and was scared beyond belief. I would test each rock, only to have half of them break free and shoot down below. Bradley moved off to the side on the glacier to avoid the rock fall.

I continued up with no chance to retreat. As I climbed it got worse. Right didn't work. Tenuous traverse back left. Leveling off. No, another vertical stretch. "Oh God, please let me reach the top". What I would have given for some snow. Just some ice. "God, I LOVE ICE!" I reached the top, spent, shaking, exhausted, and emotionally used up. I signaled Bradley to take another gulley further south; our alternative route and his first choice.

Nothing! It had been 15 minutes, I couldn't see him and…..nothing. A several hundred pound rock shot out onto the glacier. Where had it come from? Bradley must have kicked it, but was he still climbing? How could I reach him if things went wrong? 'Scrape!' Metal on rock. His ice tool on the back of his pack against granite. I took a breath.

It would be 30 more minutes before he joined me. His experience was no better than mine. Two hours later we threw ourselves into camp, every ounce of the enthusiasm we carried into the Alpine Lakes Wilderness was gone. We both quit climbing. We both drank chocolate milk. Instant chocolate milk made with cold melt water. "God, I love chocolate milk in the wilderness, why did you make me wait 42 years before thinking to bring it".

We hiked out by trail, ignoring three or four beautiful climbing peaks we intended to summit. I felt good about Lemah but wondered about Bradley's comment on the summit "why are we climbing mountains no one has ever heard of?" I don't know. Did I mention we gave up climbing?

So here I am on a plane over Idaho. Summer, Washington, and the Cascades have passed. The little mouse at South Puyallup River camp who climbed over my forehead all night is probably at work preparing for winter (as opposed to trying to get the shiny pin off of my stocking cap). My ice axe is hanging on the garage wall, boots are put away, and I have fixed the damage a good summer did to my gear. Snow will soon blanket the mountains and the marmots will stop speaking their four-word language (I can speak two of them). I did everything I wanted and more. I know Zach, Ellie, and Bradley better. Ann, as usual, let me chase my ridiculous dreams (she doesn't always appreciate the adolescent approach, though). I love her. My Mt. Rainier-shaped hole is filled.

From 20,000 feet the campsite on Kachess looks nice. I want to be back there with Zach.

*....and so I entered the valley in search of a tree.*

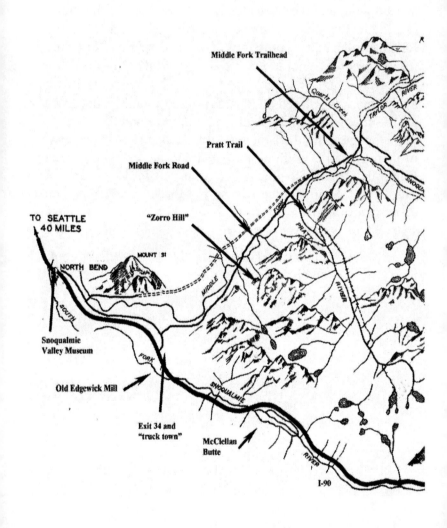

The Middle Fork Valley

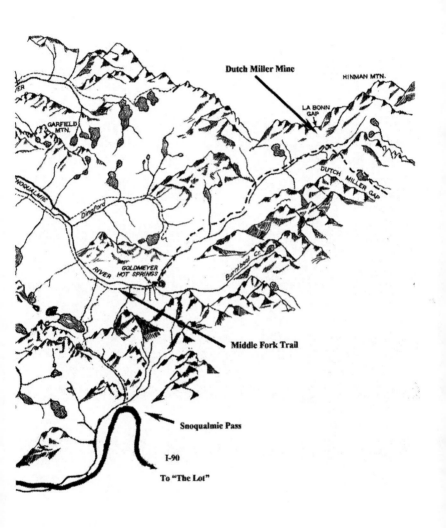

**Dutch Miller Mine**

HINMAN MTN.

LA BONN GAP

DUTCH MILLER GAP

GARFIELD MTN.

Dingford

GOLDMEYER HOT SPRINGS

Burntboot Cr.

**Middle Fork Trail**

**Snoqualmie Pass**

I-90

To "The Lot"

# of the Snoqualmie River

# Chapter 1: The Middle Fork Giant

I will never participate in the Olympics, be President of the United States or professionally race cars. If you know me this has always been obvious. If you are me, it is a revelation.

The tallest tree in the world may have once lived just outside Mineral, Washington, a small logging town northwest of Mount Rainier. The Mineral Tree was well known then. University of Washington forestry students, under Professor Richard McCardle, annually measured the living tree. Although only 225 feet tall in 1911, its top lay broken beside the living trunk and measured 168 feet. Simple arithmetic gives the original height of this giant as 393 feet. The remainder of the tree toppled in a windstorm in 1930. If still standing at its height in 1900, it would be the tallest tree in the world. (reference: <u>Forest Giants of the Pacific Coast</u> by Robert Van Pelt, p. 44).

We parked at the Middle Fork Trailhead, lashed gators around our boots, donned raincoats, and crossed the Middle Fork of the Snoqualmie River on the wooden "Wilderness Gateway" footbridge. Bradley, my twenty year old, six foot four, two hundred pound son led confidently across the bridge then turned right past the conspicuous sign warning us this was not the maintained trail.

Bradley in the lead reminded me how much had changed in the past ten years. When he was fourteen he passed up my five foot nine stature. My father-in-law asked what I thought about having a son taller than me. My response was simply, "I would be disappointed if he wasn't". It wasn't his physical height that challenged me, but the transition I had to go through as he, along with my other two children Ellie and Zach, grew into adults.

The trail quickly divided into three very informal paths. Before the timber company came through the valley this was the main path to the hot springs. It was prominently marked on an 1896 survey map of the Middle Fork Valley. But now, through disuse and neglect, it was little more than tread in places. The Pratt Valley, a three-mile hike on this old way, would be a tough challenge to get to. Today, our goal was closer.

Bradley poked around and found a log crossing for Rainy Creek. We bushwhacked through a swamp formed in the delta where the creek meets the main river. We connected up with the Rainy Creek Trail, merely a waypoint to where I was headed. I had more esoteric plans.

The previous two years grew an infatuation in me for old growth giants. Left by the early loggers, these remnants of pre-settled Washington State could grow over 300 feet tall and twenty feet around at their bases. I was looking for not-yet-discovered giants, hoping to find *The Big Tree*.

Bradley contoured around the slope and blazed cross-country. At a forty-five degree angle to the steep slope we gained altitude steadily as we went. It had been months since we hiked together. In the past few years I grew accustomed to hiking and climbing with him five to ten times each year, usually just the two of us. This year we climbed together just twice and hiked only once.

Bradley was in his third year of college, majoring in civil engineering. He was on an Army scholarship. The Army took much of his time. He lived in a house near campus, and we didn't see him much. Ann and I missed our son but knew this must happen. I was confused by how to deal with the changes.

Moving up the hill, we continued through younger trees growing between old growth stumps. Clearly logged in the twenties and thirties, I was aiming for 1,600 feet above sea level where I was convinced we would encounter old growth forest and potentially a haven for larger-than-normal trees. Bradley heard a sound, an animal in the brush, and stopped to listen.

He broke out in a smile. He anticipated this. It was deer season and he opted to not bring his rifle, convinced I had no interest in hunting animals. I maintained we were tree-hunters.

Bradley learned to hunt with my dad. They attended the hunter's safety course together. My Dad was a little disgusted that I was not taking the course with my son like he did with his son. Dad and Bradley hunted together on several occasions getting to know each other in the same way I did with Dad twenty-five years before. In college Bradley stopped borrowing my almost permanently stored hunting rifle, bought one of his own, and hunted with his friends.

At 1,600' the stumps continued. This was frustrating. My old growth survey map indicated it stopped about there. The terrain was steep with a northeast-facing slope uphill from us. This said "old growth" to me.

Not yet familiar with the logging techniques of the 1930's, I thought they could only log approximately a quarter mile from the railroad tracks laid in the valley for the trains. The loggers covered more ground than I expected using a technique called "cold decking" where they staged log piles giving them double the reach. There was a lot to learn about this valley and those who ventured into it.

Bradley and I pushed up the hill. Our matched pace kept us together in a way distinctly different than when I hiked with other men. Years of experience showed us how to hike and climb as a team. One-hour walking, a shared quart of water, three energy gel cubes each, another hour of walking, another quart of water, and then a homemade oatmeal bar. We could consistently climb 2,000-4,000 vertical feet per hour this way. This was much faster than the norm and unusual for more than one hiker. We were a unique team.

A saddle at the top of the ridge hid some old growth but it was far too high and exposed for what I was looking for. These trees were a mere 150-170 feet tall. I took a picture of Bradley by one of the big trees. Unlike my other two kids, Ellie and Zach, I lacked a good picture of Bradley with a "giant".

We violated our cardinal rule of always descending the route we came up and went down the ridge's other side, effectively traversing the ridge. It was brutally steep with tough stone finger ridges. Unable to negotiate the minor cliffs on these ridges we were forced into the gullies between them. In Washington, gullies contain thick brush and unexpected hazards. Tough places to be. In other areas, like the Desert Southwest, gullies, washes and canyons are a joy. But here they are often miserable and dangerous.

A reminder of what we looked for, an old growth log sat wedged between cliffs in the gulley we descended. Over ten feet in diameter, it completely blocked our way. Rock slides filled in beneath, cutting off any chance to crawl under. Standing on top only gave a view twenty feet straight down. These were the challenges we loved. Several minutes of scouting finally showed where we could use old branches and the cliffs to down-climb.

Finally back down to Rainey Creek we resigned ourselves to lunch. In a previous scouting trip I came down this very same drainage and found it as logged-out as the ridge we just crossed. Bradley and I sat down and ate homemade oatmeal bars and drank some coffee.

I started the day with high hopes of finding a new grove of big trees but was completely "skunked". Bradley laughed and we talked about school. He asked for some advice. It was tough to balance what the Army wanted with his desire for an engineering degree. He thought he wanted to be in the infantry but attending the Army's Mountain Warfare School and later Airborne Training seemed to temper his motivation for ground combat. We discussed the pros and cons of combat arms verses support functions such as the Army Corps of Engineers. I did my best as a former Air Force officer to give decent advice to this up and coming Army officer.

We walked out of the forest happy with the day's hiking but I knew the ramifications to my tree search were mildly dire. I thought the old growth survey map would lead me right to my targeted big trees, but instead the map was only "directionally correct". The real giants must lie in the deeper, darker, harder-to-reach corners of the Middle Fork Valley.

The other possibility was more discouraging. What if the old growth giants were long gone? I was banking on finding a really big tree for many reasons.

"Even with the cold deck, along side of a track, the track machine, like "the Unit". We called that a "track machine". He'd only go up twelve hundred, thirteen, fourteen hundred foot from the track. Then you have a cold deck there. He could go up another twelve...fourteen hundred foot... and that was the end of it. If there was more timber that way, how was you goin' to get 'em?... So you might say that half a mile is probably all that they could reach from the track."

*-Jack Smith, logger in the Pratt Valley during the late 1930's in a 1989 interview with the US Forest Service-*

Around age 40 I became aware of how much my goals were focused around my children and how they didn't address what I was going to do after they left home. This, coincidentally, was the year I hiked with my brother-in-law and our five boys, ages 9 to 17, through Washington's North Cascades. We selected a most scenic route with a full six days to make our 70 miles. Up from Ross Lake, we hiked through the Big and Little Beaver Creek Valleys, over

Whatcom Pass, around to Copper Ridge and ended at Hannigan Pass.

This journey was a bit of a reunion. My brother-in-law, Kevin, and I were best friends in high school. We hiked and worked on a number of service projects together. We shared a tendency to dream big, a love of science fiction, and a passion for faith. We married sisters and became ubiquitous.

Now, years later, Kevin and I brought our boys along to share an adventure probably larger than any we had as youths; almost a full week of blissful wilderness. The North Cascades have a reputation for grandeur but their glaciated granite peaks, densely vegetated valleys, numerous water falls, and giant trees are only hinted at when driving on Highway 20, the only road through. A few miles up the trail and one becomes lost in the blues, whites, and greens of a magnificently pristine wilderness. Sixty-five miles later I realized how different Kevin and I were.

During the first two days of the North Cascades trip, Kevin, the boys, and I hiked up the Big Beaver Valley. A radical departure from what was my typical wilderness experience, this marvelous old growth forest contrasted to the alpine meadows and glacial peaks I frequented. The valley not only *had* large trees, it was virtually *all* large trees. With the branches forming a 200-foot ceiling, the sun rarely penetrated to us on the trail below; a primordial gateway to a new look at life.

Somewhere along the trail I took a picture of the boys hiking, in line, past a big tree. Even though their faces don't show, their five backpacks formed the multi-colored 'models' for the shot. The picture was of them, not the tree. Settled into the digital storage of my Canon camera, the image rode in my backpack until we returned home.

After any great trip, I select one photo to be the new wallpaper on my work computer. There are, of course, a host of criteria for new wall paper choices; must look good in a horizontal format (certainly can't turn the laptop sideways); has to have a lot of open space (to put my herd of icons in); best if there aren't lots of contrasty lines (can't distinguish my icon herd); but perhaps most of all, it needs to draw attention. The image of five boys in front of a giant settled onto my laptop in the fall of 2005 with little fanfare.

This would all have been merely an interesting side note in my life was it not for a book by Richard Preston I read in 2007; <u>Wild Trees</u>. This intriguing book details the search for the largest redwoods in Northwest California. The largest redwood, at least at this writing, is named Hyperion. It is 379 feet tall, is the largest tree in the world, and was discovered in August 2006. That was one year before I read <u>Wild Trees</u> and the year I turned 42, two to three thousand years younger than the trees.

I built most of my house by reading books. I learned to climb mountains by reading books. Once I even designed a very robust and efficient heat exchanger; by reading books. So, I read books on trees. I am occasionally accused of living by the life-mantra "there is nothing that can't be over-analyzed." How can you argue that there is anything wrong with that? I had that burning desire now, to over analyze. "Giant trees" is a pretty big subject to over-anything.

Living in Washington State, "The Evergreen State", I not only had a few trees to choose from, there are some big ones as well. We have some impressively large trees, mostly of the Douglas fir variety. We have some very large cedars and spruces as well. Cedars intrigued me if for no other reason than the largest cedar I could find listed for Washington was a mere 226 feet tall. Obsession requires more than just a focus; it requires an obscure and eccentric focus.

Life seemed to be slinging a consistent set of curves at me. Bradley was in his third year of college, my eighteen year-old daughter Ellie was starting college, and my fourteen-year-old son Zach was in high school. I recently switched positions at work. Leaving behind a very fulfilling role, my new position was painfully administrative. To compound it all, the entire world slipped into a recession, everyone's pay including mine was cut, and nothing seemed to be going anywhere. "At least you have a job" was a recurring and infinitely unfulfilling comment.

My kids are not gone, completely. Bradley and Ellie are in college and Zach is in High School. We are at a point financially where I'm pretty sure we can pay for their college. Ann and I eat dinner alone on a fairly regular basis. I needed a big dream to fill a void developing from their growing absence.

Is the goal of post-parental life to keep working, lumping gold into a pile ad-infinitum? Is it to retire at 56 years old and spend the rest of my life gratifying some set of travel and leisure dreams? Or am I stuck working this same job for twenty more years? This must be a pretty big point in my life journey. A moment. The opportunity had and realized? Or the opportunity had and wasted?

John Krakauer wrote a short, autobiographical story called "The Devil's Thumb". It is my favorite mountain climbing story. I could certainly not do it justice but an aspect of that story hits home.

Writing about himself when a young man, John Krakauer went to Alaska to climb a previously unclimbed route on a mountain named the Devil's Thumb. The peak is a terrifyingly steep, ice-covered pinnacle in the Southern part of the state. These are the reasons he gives for his obsession:

> "Writing these words more than a dozen years later, it's no longer entirely clear just how I thought soloing the Devils Thumb would transform my life. It had something to do with the fact that climbing was the first and only thing I'd ever been good at. My reasoning, such as it was, was fueled by the

scattershot passions of youth, and a literary diet overly rich in the works of Nietzsche, Kerouac, and John Menlove Edwards.......

....To one enamored of this sort of prose, the Thumb beckoned like a beacon. My belief in the plan became unshakeable. I was dimly aware that I might be getting in over my head, but if I could somehow get to the top of the Devils Thumb, I was convinced, everything that followed would turn out all right. And thus did I push the accelerator a little closer to the floor...."

> *- John Krakauer from Eiger Dreams, pages 165-66 in the story "The Devil's Thumb", Anchor Book, 1990*

I seemed to be caught within the same grip, a need to find some sort of obscure notoriety mixed with an overwhelming urge to make life changes. The big trees had to be the answer for me but I needed to focus, a niche, some aspect of trees with the same allure as Alaska's Devil's Thumb. By the grace of God, no more than 30 miles from my house in Western Washington lay the Middle Fork Valley of the Snoqualmie River.

Known to locals as "The Middle Fork", this deep valley's mouth is visible from the highly traveled and densely populated I-90 corridor. The entrance guarded by Mt Si, the Middle Fork of the Snoqualmie River snakes along North Bend to where it joins the South and North Forks near its namesake town, Snoqualmie. Jewel of calendars, Snoqualmie Falls lies just below the "three rivers confluence". The real gem, though, is upstream. At first look the Middle Fork Valley is 20-30 miles long up into the Cascade Mountains. But a closer look at the map reveals this valley as much larger. Tracing the Middle Fork's headwaters requires looking farther east; past the Middle Fork Road;

past Goldmyer Hot Springs; past Williams Lake; all the way to the alpine flanks of La Bohn Gap, a minor pass many would say was in Eastern Washington.

Ironically, most people are completely unaware of this land beyond "the Zorro hill" (nick name for a particularly ugly clear-cut with a "Z" carved by eroding old logging roads). Exit 34 along I-90, the gateway to the Middle Fork, is known to most simply as "truck town", a collection of gas stations, service bays, and parking lots for semi-trucks.

The Middle Fork was railroad logged in the 1920's, 30's, and 40's, a romantic technique where train tracks were laid temporarily into the forest with locomotives and a tough breed of men felled and removed the logs. Logging returned to the valley in the 1960's and 1970's. Modern efficiency focused on the west side, clear cutting in all directions. When the loggers moved out the valley became an outlaw place of poaching, target shooting, and eventually meth labs; only to have the County move in during the late 90's to clean it up, grade the road, and eventually work with the U.S. Forest Service to add a new campground.

The new Middle Fork is served by an eighteen-mile dirt road that varies in condition from season to season. At times a passenger car travels there with ease while at other times a high-clearance four-wheel drive is required. Sometimes it completely washes out. Easy access brings people to anything readily accessed by the road or developed trails. But a few hundred yards off these thoroughfares is a wild place awaiting the weekend adventurer. This was the Middle Fork Valley I drove into in 2008.

I had a certain affinity for the Middle Fork prior to 2008; a relatively wild place close to home. The road is at a low elevation (under 1,000 feet) keeping it below most snow but it also sits on the Western slopes of the Cascade Mountains, thus is drenched with 100 inches or more of precipitation each year. One hundred inches of rain makes for a very wet place.

Although the Seattle area is known for rain, few people, even those who live here, truly appreciate why. There are two aspects to rain; how much and how long. Seattle receives just 30 inches of rain per year, stretched out over an average of 226 cloudy days. Not too much but really long. As one proceeds east towards the mountains, increasingly more rain falls. Issaquah, a country town that used to have the coolest airport in the world but is now a suburb with a mall where skydivers once landed, receives over 40 inches, Fall City 60 inches, North Bend 90. The western slopes of the Cascade Mountains are the home of 100 inches annual rainfall. Rain brings growth and big trees thrive on those slopes, some deep within the Middle Fork.

There are four things required to have really big trees. The forest must be at a temperate latitude. Large trees do not like either heat or cold. The area must have been missed by the 20$^{th}$ century loggers. They were very efficient. The trees must be sheltered from the prevailing winds or the giants, sticking their heads above the crowd, will simply have their crowns blown off. And, most important of all, there must be lots of water. Since I was looking for a big tree that no one had yet measured and identified as a big tree, I added a fifth requirement, it needs to be someplace someone else hasn't been looking. The Middle Fork was PERFECT! It fit all five criteria with a significant bonus added in. It is close to my home.

So, armed with my newfound knowledge of the Middle Fork's great potential for harboring abnormally large flora, early in the winter of 2008 my daughter Ellie and I drove into the Valley for a hike. I possessed one clue to the location of my first big grove of trees, a mention in the book 101 Hikes in the Alpine Lakes by Harvey Manning. Harvey was the picture perfect quirky local character and wrote many books on hiking in the Cascades. His description of the hike to Marten Lake includes:

> "A mean little old trail 100 feet short of the plank bridge climbs to awesome ancient cedars, some more than 12 feet in diameter"

Off we went in the Frontier pickup truck, the sturdy workhorse for any adventurous approach. We were dressed to hike, snow shoes on our backs, packs packed, and a thermos full of coffee tucked in for good measure. It was a tough year at school for Ellie, her senior year in high school. We talked about plans for the summer. Six miles up the Middle Fork Road, four miles past where the pavement ends, we ran into snow. Not just light snow. Not just a dusting of snow. But a foot of wet, dense, Cascade-concrete. On we went.

The Marten Lake trail is three miles up the Taylor River trail, which is 12 miles up the Middle Fork Road. An unusual situation, this was a "big snow year".

As the valley got deeper, so did the snow. Taller trees, steeper ridges, darker shadows, thicker moss and deeper snow. At first I was convinced this was the perfect excursion for an almost new four-wheel drive but some semblance of sense kicked in at about mile ten. Do we really want to be stuck here for the entire winter with nothing but a lunch sized for two high school girls and a thermos full of coffee?

No. No, we don't. So Ellie and I turned around and drove back a mile to the beginning of the CCC trail. The CCC trail, which stands for Civilian Conservation Corps, is an extension of the CCC road, built in the late 1930's to connect North Bend with the Middle Fork Valley by road instead of just logging railroad. Prior to the late thirties the only access was to walk or ride on the logging trains. The CCC road brought public access and truck logging. The trail was newly rebuilt and ready for us with a bit of snow for our snowshoes.

We snow shoed up the first set of switchbacks, me pulling at the invisible reins that run between hikers who travel together, searching for that first big tree, Ellie enjoying the wilderness. There really was no hope or reason for there to be a big tree along the CCC trail. It was on the heavily logged West side of the valley and my one clue to big trees was six miles away as the raven flies. Neither quanta of logic trespassed into my irrational exuberance. I measured trees along the way. Tall ones, short ones, older ones, younger ones. I had no idea how to judge how tall they were and was determined to learn.

Then there it was! Mired down in a swamp where no one wished to bother with it, arms stretched skyward, was a giant cedar. This was the majestic sort of tree; sturdy, wide in girth, and with limbs that put normal tree trunks to shame. Hundreds of tops leapt from the upper limbs, jewels on a thirty-yard-wide crown.

Out came my extraordinarily crude measuring device. I later determined this hastily thrown together inclinometer based on an eighty cent protractor, had an accuracy of about plus or minus fifty feet. I measured this tree at 205.3 feet. I used some more irrational exuberance to power a little dance. I easily believed his tree was only a few feet short of the tallest cedar in Washington (according to a ten year-old book that may or may not have been correct at the time). I named it CCC tree #1 and had some coffee. Ellie just laughed.

Several months later Ellie and I would make it to Marten Creek and the group of trees Harvey Manning wrote about. The road was clear but snow still covered the forest floor. Trillium, the beautiful three-petal white flower that so represents Spring in the Northwest forests was poking up from place to place. There are some big trees there. One especially caught my eye.

Once again my complete lack of preparedness hit home. I measured the largest tree in the area that I could find at just over 201 feet (with the +/- 50 foot tool). I took a picture and didn't think much of it because this tree was a Douglas fir. The largest Douglas fir in Washington is 130 feet taller than that so I wasn't even close. Three months later while putting the picture on my web site I realized it was a cedar. I later determined the tree in the picture was well under 200 feet tall but there were two other cedars nearby that do stretch beyond 200 feet, neither as tall as CCC Tree #1.

I was either lucky, blessed, or both to stumble into a beautiful old growth tree on my first trip out. It was then double that blessing to find one of the best groves around on trip number two. I fancifully prefer "blessed", a divinely providential arrow pointing towards the Middle Fork. More likely, it was closer to "inspired". This was just the inspiration I needed.

I returned home from that spring trip and started to prepare, in earnest, for the big tree hunt. Internet searches turned up little information specific to this area and the library seemed to have even less. An obscure bibliographical reference led to a 1989 archeological report titled <u>Pratt River Logging Camp Evaluation</u>. The Pratt Valley is one of the Middle Fork's primary tributary valleys and seemed like it might hold some big trees. The report was available from the University of Washington Library. Focusing primarily on the social history of the logging camps and some sort of maintenance operation, it said nothing about the old growth forests either historically or now. The camp and its resulting report were centered around a small facility called the "sand shed". I was very disappointed.

My younger son Zach said to me "Dad, do you think the reason you believe the largest cedar in Washington could be in the Middle Fork Valley is only because you want it to be?" No, of course not, there is plenty of evidence to support my… if you… well… OK, maybe. The real question I should ask myself is, "Why am I looking for big trees?"

I have known for some time that a transformation was imminent. Although it is hard to tell whether I am apprehensive or excited, there is no doubt I am expecting a change. My life so far, the "first half", has been dominated by a determination to establish myself. My determination and drive were focused on success. My life can now either become something else or end in a type-A, stress-induced heart attack.

This particular intersection in middle life, especially for men, is frequently branded "mid-life" and we suffer a "mid-life crisis". I was not experiencing a crisis. There was something oddly different about the questions I was facing. They didn't fit the notion of mid-life I was expecting. I couldn't put my finger on anything specific, so I simply went forward, looking for big trees.

I had tried many of the classic obsessions men engage during this phase. I proved that giant house projects, woodworking, building a boat, learning to ride a motorcycle, working on engines, or climbing mountains hadn't taken me to my goal, a newly defined life.

Mountain climbing comes close to transformation, but the high is temporary and I had to keep feeding the need.

It is painful to admit that what I have is not enough; I am not satisfied. Yet it is crucial to admit that something inside is causing this unrest. I had a need to find something. I am what most would call a religious person and I have been told that what I have is all that I need. I am confident in my faith but unsure of my mission. Something is screaming inside me that there is more I was meant to do. I just can't figure out what it is. I enter this time of transformation with blind faith.

John Krakauer concluded towards the end of his story <u>The Devil's Thumb</u>:

"It is easy, when you are young, to believe that what you desire is no less than what you deserve, to assume that if you want something badly enough it is your God-given right to have it."

I knew I could never live one of those "lives of quiet desperation" (Thoreau). I desperately desired transition from seeking *success* to seeking *significance*. I inventoried my gear, packed my bag, brewed a thermos full of coffee and prepared to go into The Valley.

I was determined to take on my life's middle fork.

# Chapter 2: Tiger Mountain

On the night of September 30, 1923, one of the worst fires ever seen in the area (East King County) started at the Northwest Lumber Company logging operations near Kerriston. The fire set off a chain of events that would leave a mark on the east side of Tiger Mountain to this day. A slash fire set by two fire wardens in logged off land was whipped into a frenzy by high winds, traveled across country into Wood & Iverson holdings in section 13, and burned felled timber, standing green timber, and the railroad and logging camp.

A state law required that all slash, tops, and standing snags over 25 feet high and debris left at the end of a logging operation be burned to reduce the fire hazard and aid reforestation. The two fire wardens set the fire in the morning. The weather had been warm and dry for several days.....

The wind apparently reignited the dying fires (the next day). According to the Issaquah Press, by early morning the fire had traveled eight miles into Wood & Iverson's logging operations in Section 13 and threatened its railroad, logging camp, felled timber on the ground, and standing green timber. Wood later said, "When I got there at about three o'clock the wind was blowing from the east. There were about 60 men at the camp. The camp was a wheeled camp resting on rails. The track had been disconnected where the cars had been taken off the main line. It might have taken us a half hour to connect up. We didn't think there was any danger until the wind shifted to the North and we had to get out. At about nine o'clock, about six hours after I got there, the camp burned up."

On February 23, 1925, a crew that was cleaning up rails and debris from the fire apparently loaded a train too heavily. When they brought the train down the mountain, it ran out of air and the train accelerated down the mountain. When it became apparent that the train was a runaway, two men riding on a rear flat car jumped, or "joined the birds" as they say. As the speeding train hit the Holder Creek Bridge, the wheels climbed the rails and the Climax locomotive, one of the passenger coaches, a Clyde tracklayer, and carloads of steel plunged into the creek bed some 30 feet below. The fireman and engineer jumped clear. When the two men from the flatcar arrived on the scene, all they could see was hissing steam from the locomotive and all they heard was a deathly silence. One of them hiked out to Hobart for help.

After the smoke cleared, they found that one man had been killed. A 50-year-old Greek section hand, Nick Karis, had died of a skull fracture. The locomotive was a tangled mass of wreckage, the crew coach was splintered, the tracklayer was wrapped up like a pretzel, and steel rail was spread everywhere. The wreck was cleared and the locomotive was returned to the company shop and repaired.

The coach was apparently later burned on the spot, but most of the rail was salvaged.

*- Ken Schmelzer, from <u>Wood &</u>*
*<u>Iverson: Loggers of Tiger Mountain</u>,*
*Oso Publishing, 2001, pp 53-61*

Recently I read an article claiming that "life phases" were a fantasy. It claimed such notions as "mid life crisis" are a concoction of the twentieth century; when life got easier and we became dissatisfied with it. The author said life had been hard for our grandparents but they worked through it. I needed to learn to "work through it". Oliver Wakelam and Bill Longwell taught me just that, life is hard, work through it, the joy is in the journey.

Oliver Wakelam might have been a logger. He was a grandfather, a great grandfather, and a man admired greatly by those who knew him. He lived the kind of life great books are made of. It was a time when work took a toll every day, there were no guarantees, and tomorrow might be even tougher than today. The content of his life is like the story line in a television or movie drama. A documentary of his life would require few special affects. He learned and taught a joy of life in spite of adversity. He lived to be 88 years old and died in 1995. He may or may not have been a logger.

Oliver was my wife Ann's grandfather. He worked a host of different jobs during his life. We knew him as a contractor and woodworker. He was a craftsman. His garage always smelled of different woods and stains. He built houses in the 50's, 60's and 70's then lost most of what he accumulated during the Boeing downturn in 1972. His contracting business took off in 1969 and 1970. He owned seventeen houses, soon to be completed or ready-to-sell in late 1970. Then Boeing became a victim of the recession. The last person to leave Seattle was supposed to turn out the lights and Oliver Wakelam experienced his own financial collapse. Years later, long after he should have retired, he continued to work even after he and his wife moved out of their house and into a retirement mobile home park. His little shed housed hand-tools and a table saw; a miniature millwork where he built cabinets to make ends meet. It seems to me that you should get to rest once you are over eighty years old. He didn't.

Oliver grew up in North Dakota and came of age in the 1920's. In his early twenties, he took his horses and headed west toward Seattle to join his brother, Cecil. He ran out of money when he went through Idaho so he used his horse team to drag logs. His horses died, so Oliver spent two additional years dragging logs to earn enough to buy another team and continue west. I complain about the smallest of hardships: my computer won't format right, or the bills need to be paid.

Oliver's childhood home was a farm. In 1986 I asked him what he considered his occupation to be. He said he is a farmer. How strange; that a man who had done everything else in the world for sixty years except farming still thinks of himself as a farmer. It was as if God touched him on the shoulder at some point in his life and anointed him a farmer. But was he a logger?

History can be as much fiction as fact. Stories, only half based on truth, are told enough times that they become facts.

Oliver's wife ran out on him in the late forties, leaving him with two young children. No one in the family heard from her for thirty years. Oliver's second wife, Retta, was the only grandmother-in-law I ever knew. Retta didn't like stories about "before". So no one told them. In spite of her best efforts, the stories were not swept away.

I look around and see a world of people, most of whom could be crushed by only one of the many events Oliver lived through. Families broken. Careers that led nowhere. Life fortunes won and lost. Yet through all of that, he sat in his chair, smiled, closed his Bible, and headed out to the workshop to hand craft a cabinet. At the end of the day, he fed his family and was fully prepared to meet his maker.

For many years Oliver seemed to everyone but him to be dying. I visited him in the hospital. Although this sounds noble it is probably best described as "easy"; he was at the hospital on the campus of the university I attended. He would tell me, "They say I'm dying again. But not this time." It was good for a laugh and I could tell it was true. Oliver was full of life. A person who worked two years hauling logs by horse team in Idaho was not going to be slowed down by a body that couldn't make blood anymore. He received monthly three-hour blood transfusions. I flinch at flu shots.

In February 1995; nine years after I graduated from the university, six years after I was commissioned in the Air Force; and just after I brought my family back to Seattle; Oliver said it was time to go. This time, I could see in his eyes that it was.

Once, during Oliver's final days, when I was the only one in the room, he leaned over to me and said "Brad, I don't get it. I still feel like I am eighteen, but you can see I'm not. The young nurses look beautiful to me, yet they are sixty years younger. I don't feel old". He didn't act old either. That was his most lasting lesson to me: no matter how hard life is, deal with it. Don't act old. He left us in 1995. I never told Retta about the young nurses.

During those visits in the hospital he told me stories; of farming in North Dakota, of coming West, of building houses, of cleaning the room where they kept the cadavers at the University of Washington Medical School, of rolling logs in Longview, and of dragging logs behind a team of draft horses in Idaho.

For Oliver's funeral I wrote down some things I learned from him. I was pretty sure I could not talk extemporaneously without losing my composure so I read my scripted stories and then sat down. I found out later the stories he had told me came from "before" so no one else knew them. I am positive he said he skidded logs in Idaho during the 20's so he could get to Renton, WA to rejoin Cecil.

The overriding theme in Oliver's life was so simple. You don't need to be successful if success is measured in status. You don't need to have a lot of stuff. You may very well lose everything you own, maybe more than once. Life is hard. There are no exceptions and the joy is simply in the living. Honor what is good, worship God, love family and work hard. My son, Bradley Oliver, carries his name.

My first brush with the history of logging was shortly after meeting Oliver. I grew up hunting in Washington but had a strong urge to backpack. The difference, in my mind, was to replace walking around in the woods when it is cold hoping to find something to eat with walking around in the woods when it is warm carrying something to eat. Brilliant!

In those days Bill Longwell was not the local hiking legend he is today. He was a teacher at Hazen High School in Renton and using society's typical measures deserved little fame. He had two daughters; one talented, pretty and smart; the other smart, talented, and pretty. I befriended both of them and we all went hiking.

Some people called Bill a "hiking nut". I harbored a personal goal of becoming a nut myself some day. Bill was a visionary and constructed a trail across the three Tiger 'Mountains' East of Seattle. At the time carving a trail into a minor foothill ravaged by logging and barely a few years into replanting seemed ridiculous.

Thirty years, later Bill's complex series of trails and the carefully managed state forest they traverse have become the "Issaquah Alps". They are a regional hallmark and are frequently listed first in the list of reasons why Issaquah is one of the best places in the country to live. Bill Longwell was a visionary. I liked him because he was a bit of a nut.

A hike with Bill would start just off Highway 18 and the steep drive north through the woods, up the old logging road. We would stop at an obscure straight section of single-track road. A small silver foil marked the trailhead for the Tiger Mountain Trail (the TMT). In those days, trailheads had to be hidden or they would be destroyed by dirt bikes. Thirty years later, some degree of decorum on the part of the general populace prevents the worst of the ravages.

Off we went on one, two, or three day trips towards Issaquah. Tiger Mountain became many things to me; a place of firsts, a place of friendships, a place of transition and transformation. A short trip might change an attitude, a longer one might adjust how I looked at friends for the rest of my life.

Three days was a trip with friends. Hiking as few as 5-6 miles per day, we camped in spots now obliterated by the Department of Natural Resources. Campers are no longer welcome in the Tiger Mountain Forest. Some camping spots were tent platforms carved into the hillside, others were old roads or rail grades from the logging days. The dogs barked in the backyards of Mirrormont, a nearby housing suburb, while we drank root beer from plastic two-liter bottles. My first excursion without adult supervision was a three day trip along Bill's TMT. Dave Mock was in that group, I have a picture of him eating marshmallows on the top of West Tiger. Dave is now an Anglican vicar in Manchester, England.

Two day trips were frequently with Bill and his daughters. Bill told stories and talked about life. Bill had ideas and views very different from the family I grew up in.

They did not contradict, but they were subtly different. I was challenged in ways I was not used to. Most things were very black and white in my family's house but Bill had a way of pointing out the gray without preaching. I began to realize much of the gray was important. Life was not better when I insisted everything be labeled either "black" or "white".

Bill was a philosopher and wise man. Bill asked questions, challenged you to think and then let you do so. He didn't push his views and those views were frequently hard to discern. He simply asked that, as you looked on the world around you, you reflect. Think it through. Don't take everything for granted. Don't accept blindly that which is handed to you.

One day trips were grueling day hikes. Seventeen miles. Bill in the lead, his two daughters and their two girl friends right behind, and Brad dragging up the rear. Determined and honed to hike, Bill tromped out the entire Tiger Mountain Trail in a few hours. I suffered, hounded by the fear of failure in front of four girls whom I was bound and determined to impress. How could I go seventeen miles in a day?

Bill didn't believe in stopping. Begrudgingly he would dole out a few, quick rest stops. We had a brief lunch break. He might occasionally slow his pace for some historical or natural feature but never seemed to concede any forward motion in the process.

When we ended in Issaquah, I was more tired than I had ever been, but something had changed. Years later, the ability to go miles on end would not only become bearable, it would become a passion. Just like it was for Bill.

I have known Kevin since we were in Junior High. We had a lot in common. I loved his drive for adventure. We were regularly in love with the same girls, including Bill's daughters. In high school, Kevin snagged a girlfriend he went on to marry. She never seemed to like me much. I think because I was the "competition" for Kevin's time. I probably resented her. I had a nasty little caustic streak and showed it around her. I don't blame her, I probably would have disliked me back then, too.

The night before Kevin and Janis married in 1984, I went to the rehearsal dinner. After dinner, I grabbed Kevin and told him I had my backpack and all the overnight gear with me. We should go backpacking. He said Janis would never forgive him. She would be anxious something would happen and we wouldn't make it back in time for the wedding. We got in my old Datsun truck and drove towards Tiger Mountain. I told Kevin not to tell her.

Stopping at a convenience store at about ten o'clock we bought beer and Doritos figuring those would get us by for one night. We hiked in from Highway 18 and looked for the hillside with the tent platforms, couldn't find them, and ended up sleeping on the trail. The next day Kevin got married. He did tell Janis and, unexpectedly, she forgave him. She never forgave me. The next year I married Janis's sister, Ann. Life is complicated.

Tiger Mountain provided a setting for the transformation of Kevin's and my relationship as well as a launch for the rest of our lives. To this day Tiger Mountain is a place of beginnings and endings. The Holder Creek train wreck was just such a beginning.

Once, while hiking the Tiger Mountain Trail with Bill Longwell, he took us past the switchback at Holder Creek beyond the formal trail to a small track in the forest. The bend in the trail is called Zeig's Zag on the map, a reference to a trail building helper of Bill's. A few yards past the trail, we came to Holder Creek where there are the twisted remains of old trains. I was infinitely intrigued. This is the "Indiana Jones-style" adventure teenage boys live for but never really have. Old wheels and castings, some wood debris and other unidentifiable junk was strewn amongst the ferns, rocks, and under brush. We returned to the TMT and finished our hike. I didn't realize it then, but Bill just handed me a gift; a fascination with the wilderness's hidden history.

I couldn't put the train wreck aside. Something about it grabbed my imagination. What had happened there? Bill seemed to know some and told us a little. It's ironic, that a person like me who tends to say 110% of what I actually know so admires people like Bill and Oliver, who only speak about 10% of their total knowledge. A train had run away and one person died in the resulting crash. Two people jumped off...

I researched the origins of the wreck in the University of Washington (UW) Library but could never find much. Ann and I went up to see the wreck and take pictures in 1985. We found an old enameled kettle and took it home, something we would never do now. One grows to see that most things are better left for all to enjoy. It's a practical lesson since that kettle is now long gone.

I wanted to understand the train bits and pieces we just saw so Ann and I drove from Tiger Mountain to the old mill town of Snoqualmie. Near the Weyerhaeuser Mill is an old railroad siding with a collection of locomotives and train cars from a bygone era. I took pictures of Ann next to the complete trains and compared them to the parts at Holder Creek.

At the time I didn't realize the nearby mill was processing some of the last old growth logs out of the Middle Fork. I have since learned that old growth trees are important. The Holder Creek wreck and those old trains in Snoqualmie were the beginning of this journey.

The search for the story behind the train wreck was one of the first "adventures" for Ann and me. We made a day-trip based on some research and a hunch. For twenty-four years these hunch-fueled jaunts have been, for me, the highlights of our life together. Ann seems to enjoy them but I suspect she is occasionally just humoring me. Our adventures have become more audacious but are always obscure. We don't have to find anything, but it helps.

Ken Schmelzer's account of Wood and Iverson's train wreck, at the beginning of this chapter, was not published until 2001. I found it by accident while reading about logging history in 2008. Yet, if I put the pieces together I already knew the story. Remarkably, stories from Bill and a lot of speculation created the story before I had a chance to read it. History's conduit is not so random.

There was a time, not too long ago, when men had to work hard and circumstances created character. That was common then and special now. Finding that special character provides us with the Professors of Transformation in the great University of Life. Bill Longwell taught me how to hike. It's a passion I owe a great debt to him for. He also showed me that the journey, the hike, the process, are where the joy is. The rewards are in the valleys, not the mountain tops. It took me thirty years and seventy mountain tops to learn the lesson. But I don't regret the journey.

The library at the UW didn't resolve any mysteries in 1985 when I searched for the origins of the train wreck on Holder Creek. But in 2008 it was pure gold. I was firmly set on finding the Middle Fork Giant and the task's scope was beginning to dawn on me. In April 2008 I was taking a three-day class at the UW Business School when the bus got me there earlier than expected.

I went to the library and started searching under Middle Fork of the Snoqualmie. With twenty individual libraries and over six million volumes I expected to find a list of references in the University of Washington Libraries. Instead, I found three. One was a map. I asked where the map collection was and discovered it didn't open until later that day. Class went long and I went home.

The next day class was a bit shorter. At 2:00 I headed for Suzzallo, the graduate library. The map collection is in the basement very near the Special Collections where, 25 years before, I searched and found very little on the Holder Creek train wreck. The map room is in the 'second basement'. How cool is that? I was Indiana Jones again.

I was the only person in the map room as I paged through the giant maps. The maps are as big as a large table, the numbers on them small, and they are stacked flat in giant drawers. Then, just as I was about to give up, there it was: a 1990 map based on a survey of old growth in the Mount Baker-Snoqualmie National Forest. I didn't yet realize how big a deal this particular map was going to be for me.

The Middle Fork valley contains over 100 square miles of forest, river, and high country. Since the big trees only grow on the lower slopes, I had about 70 square miles to search through. Each square mile takes days to check for big trees yet only a small portion of the total area still harbors the old growth I was seeking. Without this map my search would have consisted of endless plodding through logged-off second growth and, most likely, giving up.

The map changed all that. Now I had green shaded areas to guide me. Areas to target. Areas to ignore. I took digital photos of the map and headed home. I had the map. It was the first, significant break in my search for giants.

Bill and Oliver are both gone now. Oliver lived a long life and Bill was taken young. Although I once dreamed of being a captain of industry, or climbing the world's highest mountains, I have come to realize the best things in life are more like finding a mysterious train wreck or taking two years to come across the country to see your brother. Bill didn't climb mountains and Oliver was never rich. It's the journey down the coast, creating a trail in some obscure foothills, or living a life of such significance that your family says your name with reverence. That is the journey.

It's a 30-minute drive and I arrive at the Middle Fork before sunrise. Dawn comes during a ten-mile drive up the rutted road that lies on top of what was once a logging railroad. First light finds us hiking into the forest, a new horizon to search for giants.

If I truly understood the lesson Bill and Oliver taught I would continue this pursuit as simply a journey to be savored. I would walk among the trees. I would breathe every minute deeply. I would always take people along. I'm not there yet. I measure the big trees. I imagine how all of my life problems will go away when I find the tallest cedar in Washington. Apparently it will take a while to let go of success and truly grasp significance.

Ann tells of going to the big Western Washington State Fair when she was a young girl with her mom, dad, brother, sisters, Oliver and Retta. They were in the stock barn, looking at a remarkably large cow when someone said they sure wished they could see it standing up, instead of lying on the hay. Oliver leaned over, and slapped the animal in just such a way that the cow jumped up and stood there so all could see. Oliver had been a contractor for many years by then, but it didn't dim his primary vocation. Oliver Wakelam was a farmer and the cow knew it.

Our natural tendency is to pursue ever-increasing success, usually measured by wealth, riches, and "things". Finding significance in the journey requires guidance…a table-sized map…or people to mentor our ways.

In the fall of 2008 I sat alone deep within the forest of the Middle Fork Valley, and listed the men I knew who had the biggest influence on my life. It was my list of great men I know. There are sixteen men on the list.

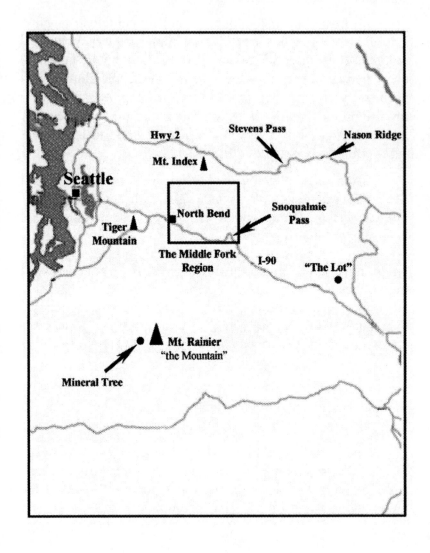

My Washington

# Chapter 3: Characters

*In the Bible, ravens are always God's helpers.*

The Twentieth Century history of the Middle Fork Valley is intimately entwined with that of the North Bend Timber Company (NBTC).

Robert Vinnedge formed his first lumber company in 1903, the Vinnedge-Murdock Lumber Co. In 1904, Vinnedge joined William Weeks, a local timber claim operator since 1889, in purchasing two sections of timber. These two square miles of forest became the basis for the North Bend Lumber Company.

The North Bend Lumber Company (as the NBTC was called before 1923) built their mill in Edgewick, Washington in 1906, creating an economic engine to drive

North Bend. People moved to the new town and it incorporated in 1909. In the 1910's, the NBLC was highly prosperous, focusing on timber at the base of Mt. Si and up to the mouth of the Middle Fork (Camp 16 to Camp 15). A disastrous 1918 flood destroyed the Edgewick Mill and seventeen homes in tiny Edgwick town. This not-so-natural disaster started with the bursting dam belonging to the City of Seattle Water Department. Uninsured losses were not easily recuperated and a lawsuit pended for years. This financial shadow cast a gray pall over what should have been the prosperous twenties.

In 1923 Robert Vinnedge bought out the majority of William Weeks' shares in the NBLC, reorganized the company, and renamed it the North Bend Timber Company. Soon after, the NBTC started focusing on the Middle Fork Valley, shifting timber operations there by 1927. In 1928 and 1929 the main railroad line was built past Camp Brown (near the site of the modern campground) to one mile up the Taylor River.

The Great Depression significantly affected the timber business in the Pacific Northwest from 1929 through 1932 with the NBTC all but shut down during those years. In 1932 logging began in the area between Camp Brown and Goldmyer Hot Springs, a natural geothermal springs next to Burnt Boot Creek, fancifully planned as a resort but never completed. In 1934 Vinnedge obtained a loan to help finance the business and then, that same year, was seriously injured in a car accident. He spent nine months bedridden.

By late 1935, NBTC loggers were able to commence the construction up the Pratt Valley. The main bridge over the Middle Fork was completed in 1936. Later in 1936, after seven dry years for bank financing, the NBTC secured key loans to finally finance the Pratt Valley logging. Logging in the Pratt Valley followed the construction of the railroad up to Thompson Lake. Logging continued in the Pratt Valley until 1941.

My search for giants commenced in earnest in the fall of 2008. The previous summer a group of us climbed Mount Rainier. My friend Chris climbed with his fifteen year old son, Marcus. The next month, Marcus, inspired by his Rainier summit, wished to learn some map and compass skills before attending a tough series of Search and Rescue training courses. I volunteered to help and we headed for the forest.

We planned to go east of the mountains where the weather was typically dryer. But as the weekend neared it became clear, or typical of Northwest weather, not so clear that the gray, damp, wet was going to stretch all the way past the eastern slopes of the Cascades. It was no use driving two hours to get wet when we could drive half that and probably get twice as wet. I intended to check out some of the old growth areas on my newly discovered map, and this was just the opportunity.

We parked my truck at an unmarked curve and went straight up the rugged western shoulder of Mount Garfield. It was great cross-country practice; steep, yet open in a fairly mature second growth forest. Large stumps were everywhere. They were the old style stumps, six feet or more in diameter with notches where the loggers placed their spring boards.

Before the chainsaw became the primary tool to fell trees, loggers used axes and saws. Since the work was all by hand it was typically easier to cut a few feet up the trunk. The loggers cut notches in the tree, placed long planks into the notches, and stood on a plank in order to saw or chop in a more optimum position. The springboards formed level, steady perches. Springboard notches are, therefore, telltale signs of pre-1940's logging.

Climbing the lower Western slopes of Mount Garfield, other aspects of this earlier logging became apparent. The stumps are large and the forest grown back with significant diversity. In contrast, modern logging replants clearcuts with hybridized and very consistent Douglas fir trees. Older logged-off areas remained clear for more years but the stages of brush, early trees, and natural re-growth produce second growth forests that look much more natural today. This particular patch of forest had been lucky, in many places the mountainside would catastrophically erode before the new trees could establish firm roots to anchor the topsoil. The marks on the map showed the old growth starting at around 1,600 feet but the 1930's loggers had been more efficient than the map gave them credit. We continued upwards through the 20th century re-growth, the steep incline testifying to the loggers' hardy determination.

The boys were surprised by how steep this forest was, forests are so often associated with flat areas. In the Northwest, though, evergreens can grow on shockingly steep slopes, literally sheer cliffs with a forest attached.

This hike was perfect cross-country training. Absolutely no sign of people, track, or trail. We used compasses and an altimeter to keep track of where we were. I encouraged the boys to look at the nuances of the contour map and learn to "see" the terrain based on the map's topographical representation. We took compass bearings and talked about how you can make mistakes and get lost in the woods. I had many experiences to pull from. Most of my "this is something really stupid you can do" were first-hand accounts.

We crossed above an 800-foot cliff and climbed a shallow ravine to about 1,900 feet. We could see the massive rock of Garfield's rugged peak through the trees above and thick forest ahead. We crawled under a large downed tree, stood up, and there it was!

An old growth forest is something unique, grand, majestic, primordial. Photos with their fractal ubiquity give no justice to truly large trees. Visits to the "tree-zoos", the National Parks, bring tamed field trips into groves of trees neatly constrained in their pristine cedar fences. The approach is controlled. Maps, handed out at the park entrance gate, fully prepare the invited guest for arrival at the giant. Step into the wild and the experience is spiritual.

Giants appear, as if from nowhere. A giant is not obvious. No, a giant is overwhelming. A ten-foot girth would span a kitchen or dining room, consume a living room, take every cubic inch of my Lilliputian office. Giants do not emerge from the earth but, instead, the earth lays out before them.

A whisper, "come closer". Another whisper, "reach out". A final whisper, "enjoy what is given you".

Reach out, touch the bark. Far from smooth, it is the skin of a mighty beast. Hands disappear into the fissure as one dares to touch the giant's skin. How tall are you, sky wiper?

There it was! A giant, Douglas fir.

Just as the old growth map's green-shaded areas of untouched forest led the boys and me to this giant tree, life demands expert consultation. Literally, we need a map for our lives. I was blessed with a father who drew a life-map for me, through the example he set, that I follow to this day.

My mom gave me a photo album when I was eight years old. It is covered in yellow textile and has a smiley face in the middle. The smiley face patch was a sign of the times. It was 1972.

Mom is both organized and thoughtful. Like most good Presbyterians, with Mom, there is a plan and purpose for everything. Mom started my album with four pages of pictures; her and Dad as little kids, growing up, later, me as a baby. I had a Brownie box camera with black and white film so I could add my own material. The 1970's were a smiley face veneer over a solid core of angst. For me, the 70's were just the smiley face.

My first pictures were of family; Mom, Dad, my sister Susan. In one, we stand in front of a sign that says "Allens" at "the Lot". The Lot was a small piece of property near Lake Cle Elum, east of the Cascade Mountains. We went there on many weekends each summer, camped in a tent, made fires, and swam in the swimming pool at the clubhouse. More than a retreat, the Lot was the soil where Dad planted the seed that grew into my love for adventure and history.

Roslyn and Ronald were two mining towns near the Lot. Signs of recent coal mining history were everywhere when we first started going there but the industry was dead. Dad was interested in the history of the mines. He would drive the whole family; Mom, Susan, and me, on old dirt roads looking for old mines, equipment, or buildings from a bygone time. Once, we were walking somewhere and pushed through a thick vine maple bramble, stumbling upon an old building foundation. Was it a sleeping quarters, storehouse, or, perhaps, a maintenance shed? I'll never know but that ruin was magic. On that day I was the explorer every boy dreams of being.

If you turn the page in my smiley-face album past the family picture of The Lot, you start to see Dad in many of the old black and whites. There is my dad with a fish, Dad at the entrance to an old mine, Dad with another fish, me with a fish, me with a fishing pole in front of the 1962 Ford pickup truck. Dad was there because I was there, he took me along. Dad looks every bit the true man of the West I want to be. Pictures of me reveal a young boy best described as "goofy" with a bit of awkward thrown in. Dad is tall and proud. I remember him backing out of the driveway and hitting the garbage truck one morning. There is no picture of that.

From even older pictures it is obvious Dad had many interests. A basketball hero in his high school, he was a starter on the team that won state. He left the Millworks my Grandfather owned and earned a degree in Electrical Engineering at Kansas University. He married Mom while he was a junior in college, went to work for Boeing, came to Seattle for a six-month temporary assignment during the Seattle World's Fair in 1962 and has been here ever since.

Dad grew up in a time when a boy could carry his own rifle at eight years old and hunt rabbits in his backyard. The backyard drifted as far as the horizon, an unbound extension of the Kansas plain full of pheasants, quail, gophers, and rabbits. He came to Seattle with the vision of hunting the mule deer of the West. He got two of them, one quite large when I was three. He took a second buck the next year. Dad was on a roll and was probably pretty sure he had a son who could play basketball, fish, and hunt. He didn't.

In the fifth grade I signed up for a recreation league basketball team. Dad put up a hoop and backboard on the garage and I played ball. The league had a rule that each player had to play a certain number of minutes in each game.

The legend in our family says the coach looked at his watch when I went in and every few seconds thereafter. At the exact minimum time, I came out. Somehow I managed to not make a single point in an entire season. Looking back I realize Dad was deeply disappointed. He knew then that I would never be the sports star he was. I knew it and was disappointed too.

Dad offered me the chance to hunt in the desperate hope that he could form me into a man. He envisioned vividly the day his son would shoot his first deer. He would show me how to field-dress it and drag it out of the woods. We would strap it on the truck and drive home on U.S. Highway 2 in father-son triumph.

At the age of twelve Dad bought me a high-powered rifle and we went to hunters safety class together. I think the day Dad bought me that Marlin lever-action 30-30 rifle, Gold-Trigger Edition, my first life transformation began. I owned a gun and had six 30-30 shells, one in the chamber for the first shot and five more to back them up.

Dad set to work getting me the gear I needed to go hunting with him. I needed wool since wool is warm and sheds water. Just as the sheep stay warm in a wet English countryside, their wool kept me warm on a damp Cascade mountainside. We went to the Army-Navy Surplus Store in downtown Seattle, right next to the Sears and Roebuck. Dad found me a green wool jacket and looked for some pants. I guess the Navy had too many pairs of wool pants that year, so he had me try on some really ugly and mis-shaped bluish wool pants. An odd-looking cut that had never been in style, I went to try them on.

I desperately needed to get rid of the soda I had in me so Dad asked if they had a restroom. "Nope" was the answer. I had to wait. I needed to go badly. I headed to the fitting room hoping I could hold it. The fitting room was sparse; a bench, walls, and an ash tray, blond artificial veneer gave little aesthetic relief to the concrete floor. The urge had gone through the roof. I desperately needed a plan.

The Army-Navy store had one of those old-style, self-standing columnar ashtrays. About two feet tall, hour-glass shaped, black enamel. When a smoker was done, they could push a lever and the ashes would fall into the hourglass, down through the skinny neck, and into the base. Desperation prohibited me from even trying on the pants.

The ashtray provided a solution to my problem in a way that needs no elaboration.

For years I felt guilty for leaving the little gift of used root beer for the person working at that store but have since had second thoughts. I'm pretty sure the Army-Navy store had a restroom and the worker just didn't let me use it. Perhaps he didn't want to clean up after a twelve year old. Poor call, in hindsight.

U.S. Highway 2 crosses the Cascade Mountains over Steven's Pass eighty miles north of the heavily traveled Interstate 90. Only two lanes wide in the late 1970's, U.S. 2 is a little more wild, its pass is 1,000 feet higher, and it is indisputably more scenic than its brother to the south. Crossing down the east side of the 4,000 foot high Steven's Pass the terrain is steep, rugged, and criss-crossed with heavily metamorphic ridges. Between the curve after the Merit Lake trailhead and the one before the town of Merit, the highway makes a broad sweep under Nason Ridge.

Hunting on Nason Ridge started early and went long. An hour before sunrise Dad and I started our day, taking on the steep finger ridges, cliffed ravines, and brushy meadows looking for the ten-point mule deer buck whose tracks we could see yet were always vacant of hooves. Hunting in October and November was cold, wet, and sometimes, really cold.

Erosion builds a consistent pattern on ridges ranging from deserts to mountains, even on snow. Mountains are eroded to ridges, ridges to finger ridges, and so on until individual rivulets carve minuscule canyons along boot-kicked dust on trails. Those finger ridges in 1978 were not minor forested hills but awe-invoking manifestations of every wilderness that was to come.

In spite of my water-shedding Navy wool pants, on one of my earliest hunting excursions to Nason Ridge with Dad I ended up wet and cold. My well-used green with yellow trim purchased-from-Wigwam "pack-boots" provided almost no heat for my wet feet. I was cold and my feet were colder. But as in any great adventure, there was a hero playing his part in this tale.

In one of my earliest memories of "Dad to the rescue", he collected some dry tinder, pulled a small axe from his pack, cut some wood, pulled out one match, and made a fire in the forest. Like some nineteenth-century Lewis and Clark legend Dad made a fire and fixed the problem. I learned an important lesson that day. In the woods when the chips are down, a Dad of great character simply steps up and solves the problem.

Yet, looking back, there was more that saved the day than just a hastily lit fire. The ability to make a fire in the woods, especially in the cold, wet woods, is an uncommon trait. Having an axe and fire-making supplies along on a day-trip is unique. Dad is unique. Prepared, intelligent, bigger than life….unique. This was the man I wanted to be.

Through my teenage years, I grew to ever more appreciate the character my father has and the character he is. His stories are thought-provoking. He rarely says things that are not thoroughly analyzed. He has thought about most things, and has an insightful and persuasive opinion on each of them. Frequently, his outlook is unique and distinctive in a way that can be both irritating and illuminating at the same time. At times Dad gets too straightforward, pushes his view on others, and drives them away.

I think my Dad is a character. I not only appreciated this, but emulated it and actively strove to be a character as well. A big part of his character is based on Dad being an engineer. Dad is the real-deal type of engineer. Function is critical, science is important, and don't come to him if you haven't thought through the concept. There is a "chicken-and-egg" question around Dad, as there is with most engineers: is Dad the way he is because he is an engineer or is he an engineer because of the way he is? Or does it matter?

Years before I attended the University of Washington and entered the Mechanical Engineering Department, Dad pretty much made me into an engineer as well. Dad taught me to look at life in a certain analytical and very practical way. He taught me to always consider the worst possible outcome and then work backwards to assure the best. It didn't matter whether you were designing a new supersonic bomber, as he had done, or planning a day at the mall, the process was the same.

Dad taught me there was no excuse for poor planning and that stupidity deserved consequences. When I was stupid, I understood the consequences. The worst consequence, for me, was feeling "stupid". Dad made sure I would never be disenfranchised and I never have been. I suspect he planned this.

Dad and I went hunting every weekend during the fall deer seasons for the next eight years. The rifles cleaned, oiled, wrapped in an old diaper, and neatly stored in the case on top of the camper bed, we drove over Steven's Pass and camped at White Pine Campground. An hour before sunrise we were on our way up the ridge, flashlight in hand, and headed up finger ridges. By the third year, when I was fourteen, we both climbed separate, adjacent ridges. Dad's theory was that one of us would scare a deer to the other and we would kill it, butcher it, drag it out of the woods, and take it home tied to the back of the truck, so everyone could see (last part was actually my fantasy).

Optimally, by sunrise we were to be high up, two to three thousand vertical feet above the highway, looking over a clearing or a mass of slide-alder for deer. Typically though, by sunrise I was cold, tired, and sleepy. There were no deer, the sun would finally poke its way out from behind the peaks to the east, I would start to warm up, and inevitably go to sleep. Who knows how many four hundred pound bucks walked through my sights as I slept. I would wake to see ravens flying around me. They were in my dreams as well. I'm not sure why.

By the end of the day, I was tired and ready to get down to the Ford and the home-in-the-woods Kit Kamper. Once we were set up in the White Pine Campground, Dad would cook dinner, we would have hot chocolate, and the camper would be blissfully warm with the heat from an inverted clay flowerpot on the gas stove. But on this particular day, I was high on a cold ridge. It was late in the afternoon and the fall sunsets came early and dusk passed quickly into darkness. I needed to get back to Highway 2.

As the sun dropped behind Nason Ridge, it started to darken. I was headed down one finger ridge and I was convinced Dad was on the next, descending, like me to two lanes of civilization, a camper, and a meal. The darkness crept into the forest, each tree changing shades of gray together. Darker and darker they closed in and played games with my soul. I saw my worst fears behind every shadow. The creeks on each side tucked in beneath me, gentle ridges transformed into ever-increasingly steep slopes, cliffs and under-cuts. Bears prowled everywhere. I saw a UFO land on the horizon. I panicked.

Running down hill through the brush, cliffs, confusing terrain, and unfamiliar forest suddenly made a whole lot of sense.

Fear filled every pore of my body and saturated my mind in a muddy, illogical stupor. This was my first real terror. True fear. I see the reaper. Yet, I'm not even sure what I thought could happen.

I grasped my rifle in my right hand, thrust my left hand out in front of me, and ran down the ridge. Blind panic.

Tearing down the ridge's spine I saw Dad's orange jacket hung neatly on the top of a young alder sapling.

There was only one plausible explanation for this; Dad was down off the edge of the ridge filling his canteen from the creek or answering nature's call behind a tree. Knowing where both he and I were, he had left his vest as a signal to his son, straggling down the hill behind him. I grabbed the vest without breaking stride.

Blaze orange vest in one hand, rifle in the other, and over-sized blue wool Navy trousers falling down my hips, I tore down the slope. I leapt over rocks, blew through the brush, slipped, stumbled, but never broke stride. Hundred vertical feet at a time, I blasted down that ridge; no dark would ever catch me. I burst out of the woods, cleared the last fifteen yards to the road grade and jumped the five feet to the paved highway shoulder. Safe!

Dad walked out right behind me, fully in control as he always seemed to be. He was initially mystified by his vest disappearing, but since I was about as subtle in the woods as a bull-dozer, he simply followed the sound of crashing brush, rolling rocks, and breaking tree limbs to the highway, his son, and his hunting vest. I sheepishly gave him his vest.

As the first of anything becomes the yard stick for all others, this was to become the measure of all future panics. Caught in an avalanche in 2002: worse. Fall from a slope on Mount Index in 2004: not as bad. Pinned under a waterfall on the Salmon Le Sac River in 1985: much worse. Startled by grizzly bears in 1985, twice in 1986, and again in 2002: worse; about the same; not as bad; somewhat worse. It was the panic to judge all future panics. Nason Ridge set the standards for life and, ironically, all those standards are good. Including a good panic.

I feel that exact fear today when the sun starts to drop, the shadows get long, and I am trying to figure out if I can get out of the woods. It always seems like a good idea in the mornings to go hiking alone. There is something romantic in the notion of being by myself in the wilderness. I have backpacked by myself a couple of times. It's fun to hike, I enjoy fixing dinner, but the panic comes back when the sun goes down. Then as now the wilderness is best shared with a trusted friend, a father, a son, or a daughter. Deer hunting was about spending time with Dad.

Six years later I was still carrying the same six 30-30 shells I started deer hunting with. I would never shoot a deer. Dad and I would never have the successful hunt he so wanted. Instead, deer hunting became the opportunity for Dad to mentor, to teach, to tell, to show. For me, no set of deer antlers could have ever competed with that fire on cold feet. I am pretty sure Dad really wanted me to get some antlers.

Dad is a hunter. I am not.

Dad is a man. Because of him, I am too.

My third intentional search for big trees in the Middle Fork was on the Middle Fork Trail. I hiked in alone to 9-Hour Creek, measured the big tree there, named it the 9-Hour Giant then, headed up hill. Leaving that 230-foot tall, nine feet in diameter tree behind, I trudged up to where the stumps ended at about 1,600'. As I would learn later, in areas where the loggers didn't cold-deck the old growth began one steel logging cable length from the railroad grade. I turned west and picked my way through the big trees.

Cliffs appeared which had discouraged the loggers as much as the lengths of their drag cables. Spoiled in the days of plentiful big trees, they didn't bother with tough-to-get ones on shelves among the cliffs. Steep ramps and ravines led from shelf to shelf while deep creek beds blocked the way. I proceeded through, looking for the big tree I hoped to find. I was on the north side of the mountain, the big trees sheltered from the prevailing winds and I was in perpetual shade. It was October, deer season again, the sun was low and it felt like evening at noon. The old fears came back and I wondered if anyone would ever find me after the bad "something" finally happened. I measured a couple of two hundred foot trees and pressed on. I have often wondered if Dad ever gets scared. He never looked like it.

I remember distinctly when I first questioned Dad's superhero status. There was a newspaper promotion when I was in high school where students could send their report cards in to the Seattle Times. If the grades were good enough, the Times would send some Seattle Mariners Baseball tickets. There was obviously a corporate sponsor, I don't know who, or perhaps it was pure magic.

I applied for and received free baseball tickets a couple of times until my junior-year. That year I didn't send in the application or my report card. I realized by then that I didn't like baseball.

I clearly remember a particular evening when Dad asked about the tickets. Dad enjoys baseball. He was at the dining room table reading the paper. Sitting in the chair at "his place at the table", he faced the family room, where I was. I don't know what I was doing, but I was in one of the nice chairs by the TV. Dad came across the application for the Mariners tickets in the Seattle Times and asked if I wanted to send in the form with a copy of my report card.

During high school the whole sports thing began to really grate on me. I realized I didn't like "ball sports", baseball being the worst. I said "No". I had not applied for the free tickets. Dad looked up from the paper and I saw in his face something completely unfamiliar to me.

Dad was disappointed. A look like a kid who just found out there were no Christmas presents crossed his face. He looked all too human, just a man. No superhero. No trail-blazing fire maker. Just a man. I was very used to a Dad who was so much larger than life. I realized my Dad was just a normal person, vulnerable to emotions just like me. Nothing special, just a man. I was shocked.

In 1984, after my sophomore year of college, I worked a summer job in the same company as Dad. I sat in an immense and sterile office, rows and rows of desks affectionately called, by those who worked there, an engineering "bull pen". I illustrated technical manuals called Software Implementation and Requirement Documents, "SIRDS". Dad worked on the other side of the building behind doors with coded locks. We all had secret clearances. We were the group at Boeing that developed the radars and electronics for the B-1 bomber. Dad's group was special.

People talked about my dad, not knowing I was his son. He was some sort of 'guru', the thirty-year guy who knew his stuff better than everyone else. His desk was ringed with file cabinets, a life's work and stored knowledge on how to most effectively confound enemy radars with electronic counter measures. The other engineers seemed to listen when Dad talked. The electronic counter measures group called themselves "Old Crows".

One day my manager's boss called me into his office and asked if I knew about my Dad. I didn't know what he meant. He told me my Dad had been offered several promotions in the 1970's. Each time, he turned them down. Dad felt that supervisors and managers spent too much time away from their families and he had different priorities for his life. Twice he was nominated for promotion, two-times he turned them down. On the third nomination, after his third refusal, they insisted he go to Boeing's supervisor school. I remember him going to school. He came back, told them his family was his priority, and asked to be "just an engineer".

They left him alone after that and Dad devoted the rest of his career to being the best Old Crow around and the rest of his life being the father who was always there.

Even though my Dad's son can't play basketball, hates baseball, doesn't hunt, and never did reach six feet tall, I know dad realizes that I am more like him than he probably ever could have predicted. Function is important. One's pack must always be full of things that are only needed on the worst days. There is nothing that can't be over-analyzed. I am a character, like him.

Dad is the "Old Crow". Crows, clever and deft, live amongst us. They are not the most prominent of birds until you take a closer look. Crows do not simply survive, they thrive. Ravens are lofty on wing and prefer the higher places. These two birds have much in common, yet live distinctly different lives.

Dad and I live separate lives. We are probably not as close as either of us would like yet I believe we have a respect that few fathers and sons share. Dad has had to adjust to being proud of a son who tackles life differently than he. I have adjusted to a father who may not be a super hero but is a remarkable man. Dad is an Old Crow and I am a raven.

Hunting transformed me. At twelve years old I walked up Nason Ridge a boy. At eighteen I confidently returned to U.S. Highway 2 a man. I hunt for mountaintops now, or giant trees, or photographs. Mostly though, I walk around in the woods with my sons or daughter trying to be as good of a father as my Dad is to me. It drives Dad crazy that I don't carry a rifle, but I shoot just as many deer now as I did back then, which coincidentally is exactly the same number as my scores in fifth grade basketball. Plus, by not carrying the rifle and those six unused 30-30 rounds, I can carry other stuff that I might need…just in case.

I thought I was drawn to the Middle Fork Valley to hunt for giant trees. The deeper I went, the more characters I found.

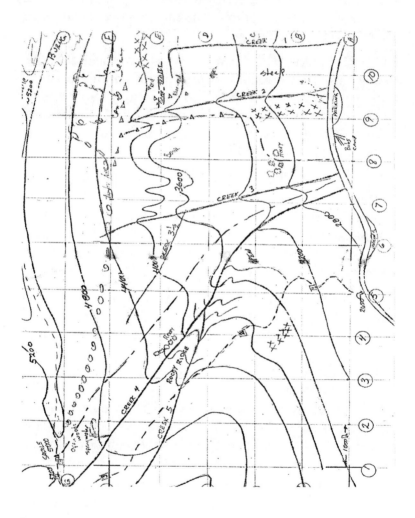

Dad's hand-drawn map of Nason Ridge. Highway 2 runs along the bottom. Between creeks 3 and 4 is the ridge where I panicked.

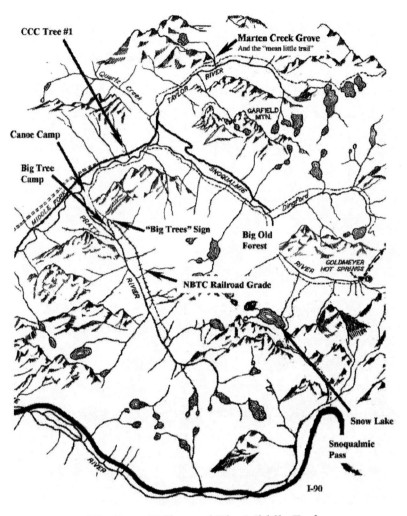

CCC Tree #1

Marten Creek Grove
And the "mean little trail"

Quartz Creek

TAYLOR RIVER

GARFIELD MTN.

Canoe Camp

Big Tree Camp

SNOQUALMIE

Dingford

MIDDLE FORK

PRATT

"Big Trees" Sign

Big Old Forest

RIVER

GOLDMEYER HOT SPRINGS

RIVER

NBTC Railroad Grade

Snow Lake

Snoqualmie Pass

RIVER

I-90

The Pratt Valley and The Middle Fork

# Chapter 4: The First Pratt Expedition

"Feed my Sheep"

- Jesus (quoted by John) -

During the late 1800's logging reached far enough into the forests that it was no longer practical to cut logs, roll them into a stream or chute and float them down the river to a mill. Loggers started laying tracks and using steam locomotives to carry the logs out of their cutting areas back to the mills.

Logging railroads were temporary affairs, hastily laid tracks snaked up mountains or through valleys to reach log landings and camps. Tracks, especially those used for spurs served an area only long enough to remove the trees. They were frequently just set on soft ground and used curves far tighter than standard railroad lines. To complicate matters steep grades and heavy loads could not be climbed by the typical steam engines of the day.

In 1877 Ephraim Shay, a logger from Haring, Michigan, built a new locomotive engine for his operation that solved many of these challenges. Three cylinders, on one side of the engine, drove a geared shaft that drove all of the wheels via a second set of gears. Grouped together, two axles were part of each individual "truck". These clever features gave Shay locomotives "all-wheel drive" and the ability to climb much steeper grades than standard steam locomotives. The suspension's extra range of motion allowed the Shay to negotiate tighter radiuses and uneven tracks without de-railing.

In 1882 the Lima Machine Company in Lima, OH, licensed and built Shay engines. Lima Shay #744 was built in 1902 and became NBTC Engine #2. This locomotive was the workhorse that Robert Vinnedge depended on in his Pratt Valley logging operation.

I was absolutely convinced that the Pratt Valley still concealed "the big tree". The Biggest Tree. All I had to do was to run up valley, pitch a tent, look around a bit and then find the previously undiscovered grove of giant trees. Then I would measure this new giant, laying claim to finding the largest tree, completing the quest, and insuring my fame.

The Pratt River flows off of the minor peaks west of Snoqualmie Pass. Seattle's main east-west highway, I-90, passes through this gap in the mountains. Named after prospector George A. Pratt who staked claims for iron ore on Chair Peak (a nearby mountain) in 1887, the Pratt River flows from the slopes of those peaks, through a series of minor ravines, to finally form a valley, which it carves for ten miles before merging with the Middle Fork of the

Snoqualmie River. Up until the mid-1970's a foot bridge gave easy access to the trail which ran up this valley from the mouth of the Pratt. In 1976 a slightly more than typical rain and flood surge washed out the bridge, isolating the trail. In the late 90's, a new trailhead and bridge were placed four miles north of the old one where the Taylor River meets the Middle Fork. The Pratt Valley became isolated, remote, served by a now informal and long unmaintained trail.

My obsession with finding a record tree lent an unnecessary sense of urgency to explore the Pratt Valley. Justified by an excuse about getting there before the Forest Service built a trail planned for the next summer, I decided I needed to go before winter set in. A much milder than usual fall gave a rare opportunity to backpack in and camp along the Pratt the week before Thanksgiving.

Zach agreed to go on The Pratt Expedition for a number of reasons. First, it was the type of oddball trip that only I would take. He likes those. Second, it looked like there was going to be some steep tree hunting. Although he doesn't like to mountain climb, Zach likes to get off-trail and "go steep". Third, and probably most importantly, it was not really good enough weather to skateboard.

I planned to take the entire week of Thanksgiving off. Work was frustrating and I felt useless. I hadn't really accomplished anything tangible in months, my boss was driving me nuts, and I felt like a fraud who, if found out, would be summarily fired. I needed the work so a trip into the wilderness had some potential to set my head straight, perhaps even providing some much needed career patience. Why not take off for a week and pretend all that just didn't exist? I told my boss "I have to go into a valley before they build a trail there". In retrospect, I would have to admit that was an odd justification for some vacation time.

Originally Zach and I planned to go Sunday and Monday. Zach could miss school for one day. Actually he would only miss a half day due to parent-teacher conferences that I was going to skip. He planned to skateboard with friends on Saturday. The weather report called for good weather on Sunday and Monday but, as often happens in the great Pacific Northwest, the weather window began to shift and narrow. By Thursday the on-line NOAA forecast called for clearing by Saturday noon, a nice Sunday, then clouding up and raining by Monday. Zach reluctantly agreed to go Saturday, not miss any school, but forego skateboarding. Could a father ask for a better son?

It had been raining for two straight months, the road was partially washed out, the forest would be a muddy mess, the weather was iffy at best, and at this time of year it was dark by five o'clock. We packed, and off we went. The conditions were perfect.

Does everyone feel an itch in their 30's or 40's to make more of what they are doing? I once worked at a company that made large bakery ovens. I frequently lamented that my life was dedicated to making sure wealthy people were able to eat a hot, fresh bagel.

Perhaps knowing that I simply made a living and could raise a family should satisfy my hunger for temporal meaning. But that was not possible because of a woman in the late 80's with an unborn baby in dire peril.

In 1988 I was an aircraft maintenance officer for the Strategic Air Command assigned in Northern Maine. My KC-135 tanker maintenance flight was run similarly to a rental company. We were responsible for the twenty-eight large aircraft during the 98% of the time they were not flying (operated by the very capable pilots). These airplanes were used for refueling other aircraft, such as bombers or fighters, and were based on the venerable Boeing 707 airliner. Because there was very limited medical ability to deal with premature infants in the great white north in Maine, the USAF had the additional duty of medical evacuation. Our aircraft had cargo holds above the giant aviation fuel tanks to carry materials, or people if necessary. In the winter of 1988, I got a call. We had to prepare for an emergency medivac flight.

Arriving on the flightline late at night, I found our fleet of planes somewhat under the weather. Bitter cold, snow, maintenance issues (these planes were older than I was), and bad luck left us with very few options for flyable aircraft. Working with the senior sergeants, we selected a plane and worked to prepare it to fly the nurses and patient to wherever they needed to go.

Sub-zero temperatures worked against us as we de-iced, heated, and coaxed the temperamental beast to life. The flight crew arrived to marginal organization and the best crew chiefs we had were still doing everything they could to ready the plane. A call on the radio indicated the situation was becoming desperate. A mother and her yet to be born baby would not make it through the night if we didn't have that plane ready in just a few minutes. We worked harder, took some chances, fired up the engines, and at the last minute whisked the mother and her precious cargo through the aircraft's massive cargo doors. I will never forget the fear on her face.

The mother and baby both ended up ok. I never knew her name and have no idea what happened to them after that night. I helped save a life and loved everything about it. That experience meant so much more than a hot, fresh bagel. For just a moment, twenty-some airmen had the opportunity to be shepherds for a sheep whose life was in peril. Where was my flock now?

Zach and I got up early Saturday morning and were in the truck, on our way, well before sunrise. The gloomy gray light deep inside the Cascade Mountains found us on the dirt road, excited about our coming adventure. Five miles up the Middle Fork Road we drove into a rain shower as the Pratt Valley passed to our right. The cold waters of the Middle Fork of the Snoqualmie River separated us from our destination. Those hundred wet yards would take four miles of road and another four miles of tough trail to cross.

We parked at the Middle Fork trailhead in the rain and started hiking across the Wilderness Gateway bridge. We were prepared for the weather with rain gear, three pairs of socks each, clothes in dry bags, and two really big blue tarps. It only takes a few trail miles in a drenching rain for a blue tarp to look an awfully lot like a castle.

The hike into the Pratt went much better than I expected. Any time we lost the tread, we simply backtracked a few hundred yards and looked for old trail tread, pink ribbons in the bushes, or a cut blaze on a tree. We struggled to get across the Rainy Creek delta, then it took just two hours to reach the Pratt Valley proper. By eleven o'clock we had set up "Big Trees Camp" and the sun came out. The sub-peaks of Russian Butte gleamed with a crown of fresh snow. Life was good and the weather was right on queue.

"Big Trees Camp" was not some wishful name I picked for good luck. There was a sign along the trail that said "Big Trees" with an arrow pointing to the right. The trail went to the left to meet the "big switchback".

The Pratt had been logged using a temporary railroad much like the rest of the Middle Fork Valley and Tiger Mountain. The tracks had come up from the Middle Fork along the south of the valley, then skirted the base of Russian Butte, and performed a huge switchback crossing the Pratt on a trestle to turn back West up the hill. Steep terrain forced a dead-end switchback before the logging trains pulled by the North Bend Timber Company's #2 Shay could grind back up the valley towards Thompson Creek. Our trail met the grade at the end of the dead-end "big switchback".

The Big Trees sign was disappointing. Pictures on the web showed a neat, 1960's era brown, wood sign with painted yellow letters and border hanging on a second growth tree. A yellow arrow (on the right of this non-US Forest Service-approved sign) pointed to the right at an informal trail leading down the grade into the forested distance, while a hand-scratched modification said "Main Trail" and pointed to the left. The forest jungle's relentless destruction of everything man-made had taken an especially hard toll since the picture I saw on the web was taken, the few remaining pieces of the sign lay on the ground at the base of the tree. A previous hiker had placed the bits, as best as possible, together to form the old sign. A portent for the trip, things were not to go as I carefully planned.

The sun disappeared and it started to rain again. Hard!

In my senior year of high school I shared a locker with a long-time friend, Dave Mock. Dave was a drummer, a dreamer, and a huge fan of anything English. The Queen's portrait hung in our locker where a poster of Farah Fawcett in a red swimsuit belonged. Dave truly believed he was a displaced citizen of The Empire. I had no idea at the time how key Dave would be in revealing the bridge between the satisfaction of saving a life and the frustration of making bagels for a living.

After college Dave moved to England, became a shoe salesman, married an English girl and settled into a career. A few years later God asked him to become an Anglican minister and he did. Dave knew when to follow a calling. I didn't see him for fifteen years.

In 2005 I was on a business trip to the middle of England, near Manchester, where Dave was living. I emailed him and arranged to meet. He picked me up at the train station in his tiny British compact car, wearing a dark coat and his vicar's collar.

We spent the afternoon at his house, a large brick home complete with kids and a book-strewn office. In the evening we walked to a local pub. After a nasty-tasting, warm beer we headed out to a second pub. Dave was taking me to three pubs that night, something he did on a regular basis.

"Brad", Dave started, "I have two church buildings in my parish. Not many years ago these supported two parishes and filled two church sanctuaries on Sunday mornings. Now I can't even fill one. On Sunday we meet in the little chapel, a few old people who will soon be gone, while the main sanctuary sits empty. England has the lowest church attendance in Europe."

I started to ask a question as we walked along the dark, narrow street. Dave observed that I didn't need to talk so loudly. It's an American trait. Good lesson. I remember it even today.

"During the day, I check the church buildings because we are frequently vandalized. Kids steal the roof tiles; we have to edge the roof with barbed wire. This is frustrating, until you realize a basic lesson."

Someone stealing your roof tiles is pretty frustrating no matter what. I hardly had the patience for this and was becoming convinced Reverend Mock had simply found a cushy job requiring little to no effort, justifying his pub-walks as work with no expectations from his near-death parish. "What's the lesson?" I asked a little quieter.

"Growing up in the American Protestant Church, I never understood what a parish was. The Anglican Church does." Dave answered as we headed downhill, a church outlined in the distance. "My parish is this entire region. Every person in this parish is part of my flock. As odd as it is at first to comprehend, my sheep do not come to church, so their vicar has to go to them. God has charged me to watch his sheep, take care of them, most of who not only don't know I'm supposed to take care of them but would be offended, if not out-right angry, to learn that I thought I should."

Interesting. I had never thought about it that way. We began to discuss how this idea could affect the American church. How in America the church can seem much like a country club. People choose their preferred 'brand' and then join in. Lost in the club, we forget those who need most what the church has. Those who need what the church has most often never cross the sanctuary doorway. It was an interesting discussion and, like many, produced some intellectual solutions, entertaining but useless.

After looking at one of his dark, lonely church buildings we walked on towards our next pub. Dave looked at me as we walked down the road and asked "Who is in your parish, Brad?"

I gave him a blank look that conveyed; "Excuse me? I'm not an Anglican vicar".....I could see it coming now.

"Brad, God has given you a parish. He has assigned a few of his sheep to you. They might be your neighbors. They might be people you don't know. I bet, though, that they are your co-workers."

Immediately I knew this was something significant. I could feel it deep inside. Something, someone was pulling at me. A door hadn't opened, yet, but there was a crack opening in front of me and I could just begin to see light. I might even have felt it.

"God has put people in your life for you to take care of. Most of them don't know it and many of them would be angry if they knew you were caring for them. Who are they? Are you taking care of God's sheep?"

This may have been one of the most significant conversations in my life. Standing there in that dark, deserted English street, my being a shepherd for other people was, at best, a dream. We visited the next pub and I met some of Dave's parish. They seemed to like him and if any of them thought it odd for a man of the cloth to be in their beer parlor, they didn't show it. The next day, Dave took me to the train station; I rode the clanking mainstay of European transportation to London deep in thought and flew home.

Although we hiked down towards the "Big Trees", I knew there had to be bigger trees than this sign promised. I was acutely convinced that since these were the trees everyone knew about; these were the trees with the "Big Tree" sign; there must be bigger trees elsewhere.

We went past the grove of medium-sized giants, old growth but only 6-8 feet in diameter, past the one really big tree (which I refer to as the Pratt Giant) and down into the valley. The treasure map of old growth indicated to me that the big tree would be across the river. Sheltered by a hill to the South that blocked the wind, there was a mini valley up high. It was theoretically perfect and we could scout it out as soon as we crossed the river.

We found a mile-long dead-end! There was no way to cross the Pratt River without getting wet. For two hours we worked along it looking for rocks, logs, anything that would provide a crossing. Crossing the Pratt would be much more wet and cold than crossing the Middle Fork, an activity we had walked four long miles to avoid just a few hours earlier. To make matters worse, we hadn't seen any additional old growth. I could tell by looking across the foaming rapids that it was not much better on the other side. It rained even harder.

Zach wouldn't give up. We kept going. At one point I went up the bank of the Pratt and walked along the moss carpet among the stumps. Zach was along the river and then...he wasn't. Where did he go? I called. I looked. I called. "OK, this is just down right stupid." What would we do if we couldn't find each other? It would be a long, cold night down here in the rain, our dry bags, tent, and dinner up the hill, lost in the dark. It's ironic how I often consider everything lost but me, including dry bags and tents that probably had no vested interest in where they were. Or where Zach and I were.

The Pratt Valley is a very beautiful place. Few places experience as much rain. On most of the Cascade Mountains' western slopes, much of the precipitation falls as snow but here, the first half of the valley is well below 2,000 feet (above sea level), the 100 inches or more of precipitation falls as rain each year. The forest shows it.

Second growth trees, merely 60-70 years old, tower to over 150 feet tall. Moss carpets run continuously for hundreds of yards. Mushrooms, lichens, and fungus of all shapes and sizes line everything. Zach noted "it's so wet the moss grows on the weeds" Too true...and there he was. How exactly he got up-stream from me, inland from the river, without me seeing him wasn't exactly clear but it felt good to see him. "Let's stick together," I said. This translates, in father/teenage-son language into "Whew it's good to see you, here's a hug."

We turned from the river, discouraged by the potential wet and cold crossing, and climbed back up hill towards the old railroad grade and the trail. The hidden draw high above the river and its secret grove would have to wait for another trip. There was another patch of old growth I wanted to check upriver. Frustrated as we were, it seemed like something we could still do. We caught the trail about a half mile from our camp and walked up the gradual grade dozed decades ago for trains. That half-mile of trail, skipped by us to pursue a not-to-materialize river crossing, would come to haunt us later that night. It rained harder and it felt like it was getting darker. Yet it was only 1:00 pm. We plunged into the heart of the Pratt.

The Reverend Dave Mock posed a question to me that not only inspired long thought on the transatlantic flight home but seems, years later, to have been a life-changing revelation. Who were the people around me who I might possibly have been given care of? Was I paying attention to the people at work or half a world away who I had the resources and opportunity to help? What is my responsibility?

It is not necessary to travel to equatorial Africa to find lost souls, to find people dependent on uncaring leaders for their daily lives, for dreams squashed by personal greed or oppression. We need only look at the majority of people we work with. There are so many disenfranchised people in the world and a host of greedy people to take advantage of them.

I want to step away from the game of acquiring riches, and supplant it with a game where I improve the lives of people. I want to provide a living wage, a chance to grow, a chance to live dreams. I want families to be closer, together. I want people to have the opportunity to provide a house for their kids to grow up in. I want to create situations where marriages are not torn asunder by the tensions of bleak financial circumstances. A noble dream for which I had no idea how to act. I wish to be a man of action.

The Pratt Valley trail followed the old railroad grade up the valley with the river in earshot but rarely in sight. Zach and I could see, in the patterns of moss on the ground, where timbers were buried, laid seventy years ago to stabilize the tracks. The trail was faint in most places and muddy everywhere. Puddles of mud and water buried the trail every few hundred yards, sometimes blocking the way. Goretex boots and ankle gators provided enough protection to keep our feet dry. It rained harder and harder as the day went on. The sky got darker and a misty fog filled the valley. Only a few hundred feet below the snow line, the wet cold soaked into our bones.

To navigate up the valley I was counting on using compass bearings from the hills, peaks, and ridges across the river to track our position. The fog made this impractical, so I attempted to keep track of the streams we crossed. I counted each stream, spring, and brook that went under, over or around the grade. During the fall and spring it is hard to differentiate seasonal streams from perennial, the map only contains the latter. I couldn't see across the valley for bearings, so my only hope was to use this technique to know how far up the valley we were. I thought I was doing ok, then I could tell I wasn't. It was frustrating. I wasn't lost, but I needed to know exactly where I was in order to go up hill and investigate the old growth patch marked in green highlighter on my map.

It is a rare moment when I want to consult a GPS. I had one for a while. I got it free for not test-driving a car. I received a coupon in the mail that said I would get a free GPS if I test-drove a Cadillac. I went to the dealer and they offered to give me the GPS if I agreed not to waste their time test-driving their new Cadillac. I obviously do not look like a potential Cadillac customer. No insult, I'm not.

The GPS sort of worked, but in those days the signal was still mildly scrambled and not all GPS satellites were operational. I could never get it to work in the woods or on the North sides of mountains and these two situations seemed to encompass ninety percent of the situations when I was lost. I loaned it to my nephew and told him he didn't need to return it anytime soon. He never has.

I make a pretty big deal about developing the skills to track location with compass, map and altimeter, not to mention just plain old woods-sense. Depending on battery-operated devices in desperate times can lead to disaster. I once read in a book on kayaking up the Inside Passage to Alaska that "Kayakers who need a GPS to find their way to Alaska shouldn't be kayaking to Alaska". I felt the quote applies to travel in any wilderness.

I do concede, though, that a GPS would have helped in our situation. Eventually I decided there either wasn't old growth where I thought there should be, or even more likely, Zach and I were in the wrong place. We turned back towards Big Tree Camp. I spotted a couple of large cedars up the hill on the return trip and we measured them. Nothing spectacular here. It was 3:00 pm and surprisingly dark.

Along the trail were some old iron pieces. I looked briefly at and thought little of them. Narrow, rectangular tubes, they had forged U-bolts around each end. Black as night, these sat waiting in the forest since Vinnedge's loggers retreated sixty-seven years before. I paid them little attention.

The further North one is, the higher the latitude, the shorter the days in winter and the longer in summer. This is intellectually obvious but the short days really strike people when they come to Washington in the winter. Add a fairly mature evergreen forest, a few 5,000' ridges to the North and South, and a really gloomy day then the recipe bakes up a striking, creeping, overwhelming, fear-inducing dark at just past three in the afternoon.

By four o'clock the situation was looking increasingly bleak. We picked up our pace but were seriously tempted to get our headlamps out. Originally I thought I could get us back to camp after dark, being we were on a trail and had lights. I was losing my certitude. Thirty years of no trail maintenance had taken its toll. The old railroad would cross streambeds on trestles. The trestles were gone now, so the trail would wind down into the streambeds then back to the rail grade. The grade and the trail were hard to find on the other sides of the streams. I felt that little bit of worry mature into an adolescent fear. In my head I was back on Nason Ridge running blindly down to the highway looking for my dad. Why could I never get past those old fears? Even more importantly, I was now "dad".

We stopped at a stream where I remembered we had connected with the trail earlier in the day. I started to filter water for the night. There was not water near the camp, other than the thousands of gallons falling from the sky, so we needed to fill our bottles and water bags to bring back with us. The filter is slow, the ceramic element took a lot of work to get rid of the pesky bacteria and viruses that popular culture says lives in the water out here.

Three bottles later and it was pretty much night time. I took the gallon bag and filled it directly from the stream. "We'll make tea or something, the heat will kill whatever is in here". Zach was fine with that. He too had the vision of us shivering all night in the cold, a warm tent, sleeping bag, stove, and dinner nearby but hopelessly obscured by a dark, thick forest.

After filtering water, we tore down the path in this afternoon-night. Only 4:15 and I could barely see. I was supposed to have 45 more minutes of light then some nice twilight. I was going to really be "dumb-Dad" the way this was going. Then, there it was. Castle of the Blue Tarp! I've never been so glad to see a blue tarp in my life. I've never seen a more perfectly set up and pitched camp. I have a lot of doubts as to whether we would have found camp only a little bit later into the evening. I could easily imagine us walking off the old switchback into the woods, spending the night shivering under a tree, then finding our camp only yards away when the gloomy daylight returned the next morning.

I subconsciously compared this event with my panic three decades before on Nason Ridge. It measured up as "not as bad".

Zach got into bed and I made dinner. I tried something new that night. I boiled water, put it in a zipper bag then dumped in two packages of ramen noodles. Next I fried four eggs in some butter and spices. I added the hot, softened noodles to the eggs and topped them with some Parmesan cheese and Tabasco sauce. It was wonderful. But, realistically, on a rainy night, coming off a pretty good scare, in the only warm place for miles, and exhausted to the bone, horsemeat in a burlap bag would have tasted pretty good.

I believe we have created a Western Meritocracy based on a hypocritical dualism in which it is "just business". It would be a sad commentary on all of us if it was intentional, yet it seems to be more ingrained than premeditated. We simply fall into a pattern of repeating the same poor behavior people committed to us in our past. A simple axiom like the Golden Rule ("Do unto others as you would have them do unto you") is modified into a painful perversion, "I do unto others as I was done to because I am a great person and that was part of my development". In the end, we create a new generation of monsters.

We focus our efforts on creating wealth. Right to historical status and wealth is given. "I am born north of The Border (el norte) so it is just that I have more". As "the wealthy", I get to decide who to share with, who is deserving, who is not. I get to set the course of those who work for me. If they wish ownership in their lives then they need to work harder and achieve it. Like I have.

Our American bent on absolutes drives this even deeper. All thoughts, all positions, all faith is relegated to extremes. I must be either "for" or "against".

"It is always good to want more!"

A subtle, uncomfortable feeling in my stomach matured into a seriously troubled heart. How had my actions, my approach, my life, affected those who worked for me or with me, who lived around me, or half a world away? In an even stranger way I felt my heart pulled towards the South. This was no way to treat the sheep Reverend Mock spoke of.

I had one of the strongest feelings ever for me. I felt there must be something really important here; something I could build on and perhaps pattern my life around. Dave sent me a book to read on serving those you work with. The book was ok but it didn't quite bring it all together. It answered some of the questions but the puzzle still lacked half of its pieces.

It was hard to apply any of this in such a way to actually make a difference in the lives of those around me. I fell into a "random acts of kindness" sort of approach. I knew where I was going and how I got <u>here</u> but the fog around me obscured the way to get <u>there</u>.

After a long but very restful night wrapped in the yellow synthetic sleeping bag, tucked into our green tent, and sheltered by the blue tarp, we rose early and went down to the Pratt Giant, the well-known old growth tree left by the loggers. We looked around and found a sign that said "Diameter 9' 6", height 250 feet" hidden by brush on the downhill side. This sign matched the "Big Trees" sign in style yet seemed to be placed to serve a trail system long lost to the encroaching vegetation.

I pulled from my pack my newly assembled electronic inclinometer and precisely measured distance line. With a newfound level of precision, I measured the tree at 10 feet in diameter but only 170 feet tall. The top 80 feet of the tree lay to the side, blown off years ago. It's a sad commentary; a lone giant will soon lose its top. Unprotected by neighboring trees or a north-facing cliff, the exposed height will eventually succumb to a "hundred-year wind", a common occurrence for a tree that can live many centuries.

In the end, we didn't discover any other significant old growth on this trip. I believed this discovery would be the "big event" in my search but it was clearly the largest disappointment to date. As we hiked back to the truck the next afternoon I reflected on my expectations. If, during the Great Depression, I secured three loans in order to bridge a major river and log a valley, what would I do? The answer was obvious. I would make the most of it and maximize the return on my investment.

The North Bend Timber Company had done just that. I would, on a later trip, discover the swath of old growth I was looking for up the valley. The trees were not as tall as I hoped and, during this first trip, we walked right through it in the fog. Four months later, in 2009, I would explore the south side of the Pratt that we did not cross the river to. The stumps went far up the hill and filled the draw, the old growth giants long gone. The NBTC had been very thorough and I admired their work. I admired the new growth. This is a magic place.

Coming out of the valley, we headed north along the river, retracing our steps on the old trail, finding the way much easier than when we had entered this enchanted land the day before. We found the clearing that had once been the site of "Halfway House". We enjoyed the lengthening shadows looking for remains of this little log guesthouse halfway from North Bend to the hot springs at Goldmyer. It was a casual end to a sunny day.

A mile before the bridge at the trailhead, shots rang out close by. Looking across the river, we saw hunters target shooting. Were they shooting over the river toward our trail? We had not worn orange, like we should have, and I was a bit apprehensive about entering their field of fire. We settled in behind an old growth log and had snacks as they pop-popped away with their rifles.

Zach and I discussed the trip. He mentioned the iron rectangles far up the Pratt. I had seen them too. What were they? I pulled out my journal and sketched, as best as we could remember, the hardware lying on the old rail grade. It was hard to remember if they had a flange around the edge. Which way did the U-bolts point? Was there writing on the sides? We wondered what they were. My interest was piqued as two more shots rang out.

I watched from a small opening to see if they were firing toward or away from the river. I never could tell but we managed to cross while they reloaded. A final, symbolic taste of adventure.

Looking back, I had to admit it was a great weekend. I will never forget Zach theorizing that the large funguses on the sides of trees were alien spaceships, wedged in place, cleverly disguised, and just waiting for the right moment to ambush us all. Or letting him wear my clothes so he could warm up only to have him say, "Dad, do I look just like you? Take my picture so we can show Mom."

The best meal in the world is granola bars while sitting on the ground. There is no drink quite like chai tea and milk soaked with sugar and slurped horizontal in a wet tent. Who can complain about going to bed at 6:30 then waking up thinking it is 1:00 AM only to realize I slept thirteen hours straight and it is really 7:30 in the morning?

I realized once again it was neither the goal nor the destination that brought the most joy. Instead, it was the journey and the experience of being with those who I was blessed to travel beside.

I returned home morally, spiritually, and parentally rejuvenated. I even found I had gained some patience for work.

The desire to do something big, achieve something greater, or achieve some level of significance is easy to have but hard to realize. Random acts of kindness are useful but frequently over shadowed by a more general life-direction of self-preservation, acquisition, or pure success. Perhaps this states the obvious, but it is very hard to achieve significance in an ordinary endeavor. That which is significant must also be hard, not only to accomplish but also to find. I was puzzled, how do I apply Dave's advice on finding my sheep?

The search for trees was in dire need of something different as well. Bits of notes, scraps of maps, and a vague urge to run around in the woods looking for trees was only producing minor victories by complete happenstance. Wandering around in the woods bumping into trees was interesting, but not getting me anywhere.

For Christmas 2008, Mom and Dad gave me a new, much more modern GPS and Ann gave me a book of Kinsey photographs. The GPS was exactly what I needed to locate treasures in the dark forest, while in the book Darius Kinsey's photographs show local Northwest logging scenes in the late 19th and early 20th centuries. Page 109 showed an eighty-five ton Baldwin Locomotive pulling flat cars full of Weyerhaeuser logs near Stillwater. Each log car carried a giant log, perhaps eight to ten feet in diameter, held in place by smaller, more "run of the mill" logs on each side. Each "holder" log was chained securely to stake pockets lining the sides of the log car. The stake pockets, narrow and rectangular are held firmly in place with U-bolts. Cast of iron, they are dark as night. I paid attention to those little rectangles this time.

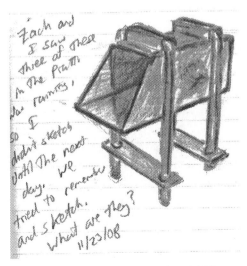

Journal Sketch, November 2008

I may have walked out of the Pratt unsuccessful in one way, but the Valley's history unexpectedly lodged itself inside me. I was inspired.

# Chapter 5: Lead Change

*Do not go where the path may lead; go instead where there is no path and leave a trail.*

- Ralph Waldo Emerson

Railroad logging initially made the forests part of the logging town's "backyard". Loggers could load up on train cars in the morning, ride to the cutting area, work all day, then ride back home at night. As they pressed deeper into the mountains this became increasingly unworkable. Logging companies wished to pay for cutting, skidding, yarding, and loading trees, not for riding trains.

So the logging companies built mobile camps. Bunkhouses on rail car chassis were pulled into the forest to house the loggers. Kitchen and dining cars would fill out the tiny cities with ample free, good food a key company benefit.

The North Bend Timber Company built camps at various locations along the Middle Fork; Camp 16 below Mt. Si, Camp 15 at the mouth of the Valley, Camp Brown near the Taylor confluence. There is no documentation of a camp in the Pratt River Valley.

It occurred to me, while poking around the Middle Fork for big trees and finding mostly stumps, that it would be incredibly useful to have a map that showed which areas of the Middle Fork Valley were logged and when. The treasured map I found in the UW library map room was helpful but at times hard to interpret. This was a convenient excuse to do some historical research on the Middle Fork Valley hoping the history might give additional clues to old growth groves and the secret giant. Maybe someone familiar with the history would know something about big trees and where they might be.

A map is more than a piece of paper, it is a collection of experiences and observations. A map is amplified by the interpretations of those who have lived it. I wanted to talk to those who had "lived" the marks on the historical maps.

I looked up the Snoqualmie Valley Historical Museum on November 2nd to find their open hours. I decided to visit the museum and meet some people who know history. The first fact I learned about Snoqualmie Valley history is that the History Museum closes for the winter on October 31st.

A few back and forth e-mails later and I was put in contact with one of the museum's board members, Mr. Dick Kirby. A note from the museum curator said Dick was a seasonal ranger for the U.S. Forest Service and I should talk with him. To my surprise, a few weeks later he e-mailed offering to meet.

We finally settled on a day to meet for lunch at the new Roadhouse Restaurant in Fall City. On the phone Dick explained to me that he was a Fire Prevention Technician who worked exclusively in the Middle Fork Valley for 32 consecutive summers, 1965 to 1997. He asked how to recognize me when we met. I said I was bald and drove a dirty Nissan Frontier truck. He said he was a "short, old, bearded guy".

The next Thursday I was driving east on the Fall City Highway en-route to the Roadhouse, thinking about the meeting and preparing my questions. On the phone Dick said he knew Fall City well since he was a teacher at the middle school there. This allowed him to work summers for the U.S. Forest Service. Two and two finally summed up to four in my mind. I realized I was having lunch with my kids' seventh grade science teacher, Mr. Kirby.

In the restaurant there were three short, old, bearded guys plus two bald guys. I introduced myself twice before I met Dick.

In general it is fairly easy to father a child. It is often done unintentionally and is regularly accomplished by even the most inept and unskilled men. As I learned, from my dad, to BE a father requires something more than the initial fatherly contribution.

One can navigate through the forest in two ways. The most common method is to use distant landmarks; peaks, ridges, big trees; to gage progress and to mark locations. In thicker forests or when the weather closes in, these visual cues are no longer available and navigating requires dead reckoning.

In dead reckoning, there are no visible clues. Walking the direction given by the compass needle is an act of pure faith only confirmed upon arriving at the proper destination. The route during dead reckoning is lined with uncertainty, questioning, and self-doubt. Few people have the determination, fortitude, and patience to do it right. In all cases, one is a little off-route. Being a father definitely involves dead reckoning.

I hesitate to describe my relationship with my oldest son, Bradley. To use "raise" seems inappropriate, since I learned as much or more from the experience as he did. I learned the role of father on the job and am convinced I didn't really start to get it right until he was ten years old. I often wonder if I wasted those first ten years.

Bradley was born in 1988 while I was stationed at Loring Air Force Base at the Northern tip of Maine. I was proud to be an Air Force officer and even more proud to be in the Strategic Air Command. Bombers and tankers were my life. Winters were cold, the north of Maine receives sixteen feet of snow per year and forty mile per hour winds are the norm. Bradley was born ten days late, in April.

After Bradley was born the nurses put him in a little, clear incubator to warm up. He was barely cleaned up from the most traumatic experience of his four-hour life and he lay there in the light and heat. Lying on his back, his head was tilted towards me, eyes wide open. Warm and safe, he looked at me with expectations I had no idea how to fulfill. My own Dad showed me the way, I wished to follow his lead.

For the first ten years of Bradley's life we spent time together the way most fathers and sons do. I carried him in a backpack until he was too big. I stopped hiking after carrying him along the coastal trail in Fundy National Park, Canada. I walked out of the woods along the Atlantic Ocean of New Brunswick and gave up hiking. Life with a child seemed to crowd out many of the passions I had pursued and hiking was an easy one to give up. I carried Bradley out of the wilderness and left behind the best place for fathers and sons.

Dick Kirby attended fire lookout school in 1965 and graduated as a Fire Prevention Technician. The Forest Service was posting two job openings. He showed up for work with his old car and headed for his new job in the fire lookout. Another graduate drove a nicer car and the road to the fire lookout was short and regularly graded. The Middle Fork Road was not. Dick and his old car were reassigned from the fire lookout to the Middle Fork Valley.

In 1966, the Forest Service pulled a trailer into the Middle Fork Valley and parked it at the old Camp Brown site. Camp Brown was the deepest camp the North Bend Timber Company had operated. Built in 1928 and 29, the camp was named for civil engineer Robert Brown. Robert Brown worked for the NBTC surveying and planning the tracks. He was killed in 1928 by a backing locomotive.

Kirb, as he is called by those who know him, lived at Camp Brown every summer from 1966 to 1975. Heavy rain and jungle-like vegetation quickly overcome and destroy most wood and metal structures in the Northwest. The woods of the Middle Fork are even more voracious. There are no remaining signs of Camp Brown just thirty years after it was abandoned.

At sixteen years old, after my first backpacking excursions, I developed a deep desire to climb Mount Rainier. It is hard to describe the presence this mountain has in the daily lives of those who live in Western Washington, the influence and aura it has for us.

There are thousands of mountains in Washington, each with a name. Over four hundred of those are glaciated, sporting at least one permanent, moving ice field. There are fourteen over 9,000 feet in altitude. Thousands of names. Some have more than one. But there is only one mountain known simply as *The Mountain*. There is no controversy over the distinction.

Mount Rainier is an imposing feature, a character in the story of the Northwest, something every person who lives here identifies with in one way or another. Sitting over sixty miles from Seattle, on a clear day The Mountain is imposing, attractive, and to those who have the bug, magnetic. I was going to climb Mount Rainier before I was twenty. I didn't.

My now brother-in-law Kevin was the mountain climber among our group of high school friends. He always wore a carabiner (the clip-on climbing hardware used by climbers to connect to ropes) clipped to his belt. This is a common site now but in 1978 was a unique statement of being a hard-core climber. He climbed Mt. St. Helens in 1979, a feat none of us will ever repeat as the top blew off the next year. I wanted to climb mountains but didn't get to. I was jealous of Kevin.

I turned 20 while in college, got married the next year, went off to the Air Force the year after and quit hiking when Bradley got too big for the backpack. In 1998 though, The Mountain spoke to me again and the dream reappeared.

Initially I didn't connect Bradley, Dad, or deer hunting with my desire to climb Mount Rainier. There were a dozen other men I attended church with who shared my dream of climbing, so we got together and developed a plan to train for and climb Mount Rainier. I literally roped this group in yet didn't know the first thing about ropes (or ice axes or carabiners or belays or knots).

I needed to learn the ropes of climbing. That required a partner. Bradley was ten and I conscripted him as my mountain climbing, crash-test-dummy. He thought we were going hiking.

Bradley's and my first excursion was to McClellan Butte, a very visible, pointed peak along I-90 near Snoqualmie Pass. McClellan Butte has a nice, five mile trail almost all the way to the top. We, in a way that would become more typical as our climbing developed, elected a more esoteric route. We climbed the route used by the first people to climb decades before, straight up the East side. This route was certainly not hard, by climbing standards. I was comfortable doing it by myself but we used ropes and harnesses in an attempt to figure out what exactly they were for.

The approach hike consisted of three fairly steep trail miles. Bradley, at that time a typically awkward ten-year-old, huffed, puffed, and whined incessantly. At about mile two I had had enough. "Would you do that belly-aching in front of your friends?" I said in a seriously vintage-Dad sort of way.

Bradley answered with a timid "no".

"Well don't do it with me. Man-Up and hike this hill!" I set the bar and the expectations were clear. This would have never worked if Ann were along. Mom's are like that. They are sympathetic and nurturing. Something I was definitely not, at whining mile two.

Bradley dug deep and found more mental and physical reserves than he thought he had. Two hours later we stood on the top. He hasn't complained since. On the way down, he slipped and fell on some ice and slid right off a little cliff. He disappeared. Providentially, we were still roped together. The rope went tight with a jerk.

I didn't hear anything. I yelled to Bradley, twice. Finally he called back, "Dad, I'm hanging in mid-air, could you let me down?" Coming down that mountain, Bradley wasn't a crash-test-dummy, he was my climbing partner. We found the "bond of the rope".

I stopped my rapid fire questioning and gave Kirb time to finish his hamburger. The Roadhouse served a good burger; big, rich, simple, with a liberal side of fries. As he finished the last bite he looked at me and gave me one more off-hand story.

In 1976 he, for whatever reason, hiked up from I-90 to Thompson Lake. Then he followed an old, probably long-lost, informal trail down to the Pratt River, the lower half along the termination of the old North Bend Timber Company rail spur. Reaching the main grade, the rails gone for 30 years, he headed downstream towards the Middle Fork. Somewhere along the line he looked uphill and saw a rail car.

The sight of a railcar in the woods was not unknown, but certainly uncommon, especially several hundred feet up from the main rail bed. For whatever reason, he kept moving and didn't investigate. Upon returning to the main part of the valley, he began to question what he saw. Later, he was able to talk to some people involved with the Civilian Conservation Corps in that area and they confirmed there had been a rail car there long after the tracks were pulled. It was hoisted up the hill using a donkey engine and used as a bunkhouse. It must have just been too inconvenient to skid it back down the hill and re-load onto railroad cars.

"I can't see why it wouldn't still be there, unless someone packed it out", he said. We both laughed.

When I got home I e-mailed another contact who was a Search and Rescue specialist for the Middle Fork. He had a stash of old maps and documents that he reluctantly shared. I was just starting to gain his confidence. I resolved to forge deeper into the history of the Valley and asked him for some information from his maps. He said "no".

In 2000 I climbed Mount Rainier, fulfilling a twenty-year dream. I committed that I was only going to climb this one mountain then return to simple hiking. Unexpectedly I found there was a mountain-sized hole inside me. I thought Rainier would fill that hole but there must have been a leak; it needed regular refills. Bradley enjoyed the climbing so we continued to climb together. Each time we upped the ante a little.

At first I committed to never climb anything I wasn't comfortable climbing alone. But simple scrambles led to rock climbing which became steeper and steeper. Short steps gradually became cliffs, all of which seemed incrementally do-able. I needed a backup, a safety line, so I taught Bradley how to belay.

Belaying is the technique where one climber controls the rope such that, if the other falls, they are safely caught. On our first climb, Chair Peak, that required a belay I looked Bradley in the eyes and said, "Do you understand that my life is in your hands? You screw up, I die."

"Yes Dad", was my twelve-year-old son's reply.

As we climbed more and more mountains, I caught him from time to time. He would slip and fall, the rope would go tight, and it would catch. At first it was just a nudge, his eighty pounds barely budged me. As he got bigger, the falls pulled harder, but came less often. Tied to me, he was safe.

The year Bradley turned sixteen was marked by an even more important moment. An event I will always remember as "the lead change". I would like to say I planned this moment to celebrate my son becoming a man, but like many great things in life, that moment came without warning.

It was Easter Sunday, 2004. Bradley and I started early, around 3 a.m., from the campground at Yosemite on our hike to the base of Half Dome. Our route would take us up the West side of the mountain, then return down the more tame "cable route" on the East. This traverse would begin with an 8-pitch technical rock climb called Snake Dyke. Long gone were the scrambles and simple mountain steps, this was full-on alpine rock climbing.

The first couple of pitches (a climbing term for the section of a route that is one rope length long) went smoothly. I strayed off route for a while but some deft spider-man moves kept me going to reclaim the easier sections. Sunrise caught me leading the third pitch. I acknowledged Easter by yelling to Bradley the ancient Christian call "He has Risen!" Bradley returned with an affirmation from a hundred feet straight below. Almost routinely he responded "He has risen Indeed! Climb On!" A most glorious place to celebrate history's most glorious event.

By the fourth pitch I was tired and the climbing wasn't getting any easier. The months before had been spent practicing on a local climbing rock with a 25-pound pack (the only guy around the artificial crag at Marymoor Park with rock shoes, shorts, chalk bag, and a paving brick) but the off-route work pushed me harder than I expected. The end of the fourth pitch was a "hanging belay": no place to sit, I hung from my harness, the ropes dangling in mid-air below. My legs burned and my muscles cramped. When Bradley got to me, I told him "I can't lead anymore".

Bradley had never led before. Leading is tough. When following in rock climbing, as Bradley always did, a climber is "top-roped". The belaying partner, having just led the pitch, is above and the rope comes down to the climber. A slip or fall results in simply taking up the slack and a quick catch by the rope. It's easy, and sometimes fun to fall when following. Leading is different. The lead climber selects the route and places climbing hardware in the rock. They pay for their mistakes with real falls. A slip five feet past the last piece of climbing hardware results in a ten-foot fall. Ten feet past and payment is a twenty-foot fall. Hope there is nothing to hit. Falling five feet is rough, falling twenty is sheer terror. In true alpine climbing the simple rule is: don't fall.

Bradley looked at me, said "OK", took the climbing rack (a sling with the hardware that the lead climber carries) and took off above me. It was his first lead. It was not on some practice rock or concrete "crag" but mid-climb on one of America's most spectacular cliffs. Dad was tired and his son took up the slack. The lead changed. Bradley didn't flinch, question, or look back. I belayed and then I followed.

Many things began to change after that fifth pitch on Snake Dyke. Bradley led more. Within two years he was doing most of the leading. Later that summer he caught me in an inadvertent fall and truly saved my life. He remembered the talk, and he didn't "screw up".

By the end of 2004 I stopped calling him "Rock BOA" (a play on his initials, Bradley Oliver Allen) and started calling him "Lead Dog". "Unless you are the lead dog, the view never changes".

Four years later he would lead a group of men climbing Mount Rainier. It was his sixth summit of that mountain and a tough climb. I followed all day.

Climbing with Bradley proved what my Dad taught me. Raising kids is about time together. Some, if not most, of that time must be in a pursuit where you are in it on the same level. Yes, I'm still the father, but we are both climbers. Bradley saw me tired, elated, beat, and victorious. He saw me lose my temper and lose our way. He saw me lead hard pitches and guide groups through thick fog on featureless glaciers. We talked about what was important and became better men together.

The hardest climb Bradley and I ever attempted was the North Tower of Mount Index along Highway 2 in Washington. I failed on two previous occasions and had been training three years to get ready for it. We left the car at 3:00 PM and didn't return until 7:00 PM the next day. What sleep we could get was on a ledge the size of a coffee table. A coffee table that must be shared and has sheer cliffs on three sides. The climbing was hard, for me, and the route finding very tough. We were exhausted much of the time and thirsty but there was no water besides what we carried.

Coming down we made one really dicey traverse on a ledge angled down 45 degrees with a few hundred feet of vertical cliff below. I led around it and Bradley followed. As he came around I saw him tired for the first time in years. He even seemed a bit scared. "Just don't let me fall, Dad, just don't let me fall." The look in his eyes was deeper than usual. He needed something that I had and I provided it. We made it safely down.

What he needed wasn't an axe to cut wood or a bonfire for cold feet. Call it reassurance. Call it safety. But for an unusual moment Bradley simply needed. I knew I had done it. When the chips were down, I was a Dad.

*"Lead Change"* sketched in 2004

Dad's life-gift to me was more than the time we spent together. Dad shared a collection of journeys, hours, and adventures that gave us the opportunity to show and discuss life's lessons. I have attempted to do the same with my kids. When people ask what the secret is to getting kids through middle school and high school I tell them it is spending time with them doing something. It can't just be shuttling them around and it can't be doing things where the parent is always in some sort of authority position. Growth occurs in activities that allow the son to see the dad as a person and for the dad to honor the son as a man. It needs to be the kind of activities that involve a journey, a fire for cold feet, and, eventually, a lead change.

I honestly believe it takes more than hours, it takes days together. A trip to a ballgame is fun, four days together in the same tent is potentially life changing. Eating homemade oatmeal bars on an alpine ledge watching the sunset halfway up a mountain is pure magic. Dad formed my life through extended weekends fishing and hunting together. He created in me a map that guides me through life and, with definitive direction, has pointed me towards a higher calling in the second half of my life.

My lunch with Dick Kirby started to bring things into focus: the post holder, the train car, the history. I was having a hard time tearing myself away from old pictures and was checking out books from the library on local history. I was becoming captivated by the history of this area and the people who lived it.

Perhaps even more intriguing was how little historical material I was able to collect on the Middle Fork. My original intention, to use the historical information to help locate old growth groves, morphed into seeking historical relics in the same goal-oriented game I was playing with the trees. But then that transformed into a fascination with the people who lived and worked here in the hundred years before I stumbled on to my first big tree. I could faintly hear voices in the valley.

Later in the year, after the valley filled with snow and the December flood washed out the road, I rode my bike seven miles on the icy road then walked a couple of miles to the Middle Fork trailhead. I switched on my new GPS and followed the little arrow directly to the abandoned and almost collapsed Taylor Ranger Guard Station.

The trail was several hundred yards up the hill, re-routed to keep casual hikers away from this relic. I walked around the old building, the wood gray with age, most planks still sturdily in place. The corrugated steel roof hung in tatters. Its beams had collapsed into the interior. An old wood-burning stove sat within, trapped by the fallen roof.

I had the distinct feeling I wasn't supposed to be here.

# Chapter 6: Clear Cut

*"When the situation is hopeless,
there's nothing to worry about."*

Edward Abbey

In the 1960's, a temporary bridge was built over the
Middle Fork River at the mouth of the Pratt Valley. The
logging company built a road and logged north along the
other side of the river. Some of the last old growth trees in
the Middle Fork were sold by the U.S. Forest Service and
harvested. Logging trucks rolled down the road all day long,
some practically overloaded with single-log loads. A twelve-
foot diameter stump squats, hidden by brush where the old
grove stood. Under the watchful eye of the US Government,
the logging company finished their business, planted
hybridized Douglas firs, sprayed with insecticide to protect
their new crop, removed the temporary bridge and left.

That grove of old trees would have been along the Pratt Valley trail. An easy day hike, a short drive from Seattle, a reminder of the days when the entire valley was a forest of giant trees. Times had changed in thirty years and we were wrong to sell that grove. It was a treasure that literally takes a thousand years to replace.

Simple answers are predominantly illusions, life is complex, and the solutions to tough questions are just as tough. A logging clearcut scars the land in much the same way that lives are scarred by seemingly insurmountable emotions. Sometimes we are called on to help those with issues we can't understand. These opportunities, to help others in ways we do not yet fathom, can become the foundations for life's greatest moments.

My search for undiscovered trees became increasingly murky. Perhaps it was the typical Washington winter "blahs" or simply the physical obstacle that snow and washouts created making it hard to get into the Middle Fork Valley.

In two months, I only went up the Valley once. At first I wrote it off as being "one of those winters". Tough weather was as hard on me as it was on the old loggers. I was uncharacteristically attracted to the warm indoors. I attempted to learn more about local history.

As I wallowed around in a mire of Middle Fork history I increasing lost sense of the mission, the purpose of my quest. Randomly gleaning excerpts from this book or that, surfing history websites, or the occasional discussion gave me little sense of direction, let alone significance. In addition, there was a certain haze, a malaise surrounding the whole affair.

In 2004 Ellie and I sat in a small tent pitched on a glacier at just over 9,000 feet on Mount Rainier. Called Emmons Flat, this high-altitude camp lacked the comfort features of the more formal camps like Camp Muir or Camp Sherman. The glacial camp isn't very flat. Just a short distance below camp, anything which slides away from camp goes off an ice-cliff.

Little Tahoma, the broken volcanic rock, sub-peak of Mt. Rainier, sits a short mile away from Emmons Flats as the raven flies. The evening freeze was pushing rocks off its North Face. The crashing rocks and echoing slides provided an eerie soundtrack to the pre-climb fears climbers like me tend to harbor. Ellie looked at me and said "Dad, I'm scared". She was only fourteen and her hands shook visibly.

Ellie had finished eighth grade and was at the top of her game. She was good at soccer and played on both the school team and a local select team. Her grades were excellent. She was the picture of athletic health. Climbing Rainier is no easy task and is certainly an uncommon pursuit for an eighth grade girl. Ellie was confident in her preparation. She was enjoying the climb and proving something to herself and others.

It was six o'clock in the evening. We were bedded down to get some rest before we entered the "upper mountain" where the "real climbing" began. We would depart camp around midnight. Bradley and Paul, a long-time climbing partner who climbed Rainier with me before, were in the tent next to us. Rocks kept falling from Little Tahoma, a loud rumble to the ears, a sonic-boom to the psyche. I could sense Ellie was bothered. The glacier groaned; a low, moaning creak caused by the icy base scraping on the bedrock hundreds of feet below our tent. Our camp moved slowly down hill with the glacier, micro-inches at a time. A glacial crack, a crevasse, was larger somewhere up the slope from us. Ellie looked at me, increasingly unsure of herself.

The first 9,000 feet of any Mt. Rainier climb has some apprehension; the ride in the car, the hike up the trail, the initial snow and ice. As evening sets in, as the mountain shadow grows to envelop camp, as temperatures plunge below freezing, the little demons of fear start to stir. The same bears and aliens that stalked me on Nason Ridge arrive promptly the night before a climb in the forms of falling rocks and tumbling ice. There is no sleep while wrapped in their sounds, the threats they whisper and shout. There is a climbing joke that you carry a tent so you can lie down and "pretend to sleep" the night before a big climb. It was true that night.

Ellie sat up, wearing her climbing clothes sans boots inside her sleeping bag. She held both hands up. They shook, the subtle shake of inward fear mixed with the uncontrolled shake of primal fear. I held out my hands next to hers and said, "We are all scared, it's part of the game." My hands, too, visibly shook. "You have to manage the fear".

Ellie overcame the fear that night, relaxed, laid down, and easily summitted Rainier the next morning. It was a big accomplishment for her and this was recognized when she told the story. She said she enjoyed the climb but it was the hardest thing she had ever done. She felt no interest in ever climbing a mountain, let alone The Mountain, again. Although she seemed to have proved a maturity and bravery far beyond her years, the next few months of her life were dominated by fear.

Over the next year, Ellie plunged into a darkness that tested her will, her faith, and her direction. Ellie's cloud moved into our family and cast doubt on who Ann and I are, both as parents and as husband and wife. I learned that any success I felt from guiding Bradley through adolescence had little practical application with Ellie. Ann and I held every opportunity to fail as a family.

Looking back, there is more clarity now than I ever felt at the time. I went in to Ellie's high school years feeling I knew what to do and three years later realized I didn't need to. But at the time the situation was murky. There was no clear direction, just fear like that dread when boulders crash down mountain slopes near camp.

Ann and I were married in 1985 while I was still in college. I first asked her out two and half years before. She tells our friends she was afraid to say "yes" because she knew if she did she would end up marrying me. She knows me better than anyone else but still can't figure me out. We are different in as many ways as we are similar but few people would argue that we are not made for each other.

Ann and I strengthened each other over our twenty years of marriage, although they were never easy. A series of arguments after two years showed both the youth and honeymoon were over. At seven years, the stress of having two little kids and me leaving the Air Force sent us into the worst strife of our first two decades together. Marriage was never easy for us. I believe it is hard for everyone. We work every day to keep it together.

In 2000 Ann and I rebuilt our house. Doing most of the work ourselves, we tore much of the structure apart, doubling the size and adding a second floor, all while living inside. A tough recession in the construction equipment business, which I was in, made it even harder. Still, we both understood the issue: we simply needed to work together to finish the project. We did, and coming out of that experience, thought we had marriage figured out. Ellie's bed was relocated through seven different places during the time we worked on the house, once even under the stairs. We bragged about how resilient she was. We didn't know anything.

At first, high school seemed perfect for Ellie. New friends, breaking free of middle school, and a high school soccer team were exactly what she needed. Soccer started in fall and that was when something started to change. Perhaps it was the number of talented players on a high school team compared to what she was used to; perhaps it was simply that soccer wasn't her thing. Whatever it was, Ellie began to shrink into a shell. It was subtle at first. She would sit on the sidelines during the game, her sweatshirt hood pulled over her head, a small, dark cave to retreat into. Her freshman year came and went. We were convinced that we avoided the whole "high school girl thing". In retrospect we missed the warning signs. Had we seen them, it wouldn't have changed a thing.

Ellie found a fascination for clothes and style. Women's magazines began to arrive and lay strewn around the house. She cut out the pictures and concentrated on how she could look more like them. Her five foot six frame was athletic, but her muscular form brought a density that didn't fit the standard body mass charts. The magazine articles convinced Ellie she must be overweight. Insensitive friends made comments about the numerical value of her weight without seeing the "Ellie" they represented. Ellie meticulously disciplined herself to lose a few pounds, determined and driven as in all other aspects of her life. Her life direction seemed to merely swerve away from sports and towards a new horizon, one typical for a girl her age.

As a father, I was not concerned, remembering my sister going through a similar change in values as she transitioned from a life of sports to one of cheerleading and dance.

As much as I loved bragging about Ellie's hiking and climbing, I was pleased as a father to have a beautiful daughter. Makeup, clothes, and new hairstyles changed Ellie on the outside while her inside struggled. Perhaps her friends sensed the transition in her soul; perhaps they saw it was not a positive change. Whatever it was, her friends withdrew. Ellie was struggling to see where she was going.

On the outside, Ellie physically shrank away, caught in a perversion of societal beauty values around thin-ness. Fifty pounds lighter, on a frame that was fine where she was before, everyone could see the problem and knew how to solve it for her. I was to learn that fixing the symptom does not fix the problem. She could not "just eat more".

Ann was there for Ellie but as the darkness stayed longer, months, it wore greatly on Ann. We all fight a dark cloud from time to time, but I believe they come to Ann on a regular basis. Seeing the pain in Ellie, she started to fight the battle for two. Ellie never stopped talking to us, never stopped coming to us.

Almost every week, Ellie and I would run together at least once. The six hundred acre green space behind us, a tree farm saved from the developmental sprawl we were used to everywhere else, it makes our house a haven from the rest of Seattle's eastern suburbs. Ellie and I would run back through the woods, then into the Carnation Valley. When we prepared for climbing Rainier, the runs got longer, as many as ten miles; into the valley, over Tolt Hill, into the next valley, back up to our house. When Ellie quit soccer and lost interest in a life focused on uber fitness, our runs shrank to two, three, maybe four miles. Long distances for most people but it was well off our pace. We still talked while we ran.

When we moved into our house twelve years before, in 1993, the trees in the forest behind us were saplings growing in a clear-cut wasteland. It was mostly marsh. Water and frogs were everywhere. The trees were only a few inches in diameter and 10-15 feet tall. Time grew the trees, their larger mass required more water so they drank so much the swamp dried and a more mature forest began to take shape. Frogs became less common but deer, coyotes, and cougars moved in. The trees raced to the sun and our run became a shaded haven. Just a few hundred yards from our tract of houses it feels like wilderness. The rules between father and daughter were different here and I was surprised at Ellie's candor as she shared her thoughts, fears, and life on our runs through these woods.

Ellie spoke about her fears and I tried to listen. A life-long know-it-all, I was consciously trying to learn to listen better. I desired to see things through others' eyes. This was not easy or natural for me. It was one thing to attempt to understand the business people, mostly men, around me, but quite another to understand the mind of a teenage girl. It was a quantum leap in empathy to feel her pain.

Ellie's fears were frequently generic, no specific boogie-man. Unlike the fears raised by rocks falling off the face of Little Tahoma, these fears were faceless, shapeless and undefined. They were a dark closet harboring a host of evil monsters, none of whom ever showed themselves long enough to be identified. At first I would attempt to convince her that her problems were small, manageable. I carelessly threw-out possible ways to address them. I presented to her "the solutions", just as men typically do.

My solutions were exactly what she didn't need. Her fears were not just tangible, they were overwhelmingly real. Crushing boulders, they fell like meteorites from the sky at unexpected, but shockingly regular intervals. During the day she leapt constantly to avoid being struck. But at night, when her darkness was compounded by the physical black of the night, they crushed her. Night after night it got worse. There was no future for her. She told us how she was someone with no place in anyone's life.

Ellie would come into our bedroom, fear painted on her face. It was a different fear than I had seen before. Instead of the physical fear found on mountains, this was the spiritual fear found in churches. I knew some of that fear, the "my soul is doomed to hell" type but suppressed it through an amateurish but consistent faith. I couldn't just hold my shaking hand next to hers and solve the problem. Sharing her pain didn't fix it. At night she sometimes shrieked.

Ann, who so desperately needed the sleep, would get up and patiently sit with Ellie in her room. Sometimes they would play games, or talk, or Ann would just sit, hold, and protect her. The terror in Ellie's face got worse and worse. She would come to me first; perhaps just because my side of the bed was closest to the door, I would do triage then Ann would take over. We were fighting a hasty and poorly led retreat, losing battles in a war that seemed set to overwhelm us. Ann and I prayed and God seemed to leave us alone.

This story has many facets. By day, Ellie was doing well in school. She seemed to have friends and came to church with us. Without warning, she joined cheerleading tryouts halfway through her junior year and made the team.

It was next to impossible to discern what to do. I knew with certainty Ellie's fears were real. There was a monster, Ellie knew it, and I started to catch glimpses of it from time to time. Seeing 'the beast' was a break-through, God was providing me empathy for Ellie. The monster peaked around the corner; grimaced, snarled, and I shrunk back. There was a hint of a cloud.

Ann slipped into despair. At the same time I fell into a similarly dark hole. My business travel schedule, where I was gone at least half of the time; provided a convenient yet justifiable excuse for Ann and me to slip into our respective shells. We talked less and became more like Ellie, lost in a vacuum and resigned to a self-imposed malaise. We failed to realize what we intellectually knew so well; we could not solve the problem but we could let it go and it would be solved. We didn't let go.

There is a cloud, call it depression, call it loneliness, call it demon possession, call it whatever, but there is a cloud that will envelop human souls. A cloud of hopelessness. A cloud of despair. The cloud will not "just go away". I never saw or understood this before Ellie. I saw it through her eyes and it terrified me by proxy.

While out running with Bradley one day, I attempted to explain it to him. I tried to explain the abhorrence of one's own body; the need to feel accepted, the revulsion Ellie felt when she looked in the mirror. I talked it through and saw no answers. But I seemed to finally see the question. My heart went out to those who hurt. It was not about "manning up"; it was about coming to terms with complex questions for which the answers may never be known. I was starting to see the comfort comes not in knowing the answer but in becoming comfortable with the question.

Ann recalls that during this time, she was home alone sitting at our kitchen island. It was dark and she was crying, suffering through her daughter's pain as only mothers can. She called out to God. He answered. "Ellie will be OK", the voice said. An audible, out-loud, real voice. Ann realized at that moment who could solve the problem and who couldn't. She let the problem go.

The spring of 2006 did not brighten Ellie and her pain continued. Sometimes she was up, others she was down. But mostly she was down. Friends no longer called and her health slipped away. During Spring break we took a trip to the desert Southwest. Our best vacations were in the desert and only two years before the five of us bonded during three weeks in this beautiful area. This time, instead of loving this wilderness, something she always relished, Ellie hated every minute of it. Hiking was no longer a haven for her, it was a hell. The last few days she spent in the hotel room with Ann. Bradley, Zach, and I attempted a long cross-country route in Zion National Park but a storm moved in and killed our plans. We returned a day early to the hotel and sat in the hot tub as the thunder and lightning ended our vacation. As night closed in we could see the darkness around Ellie.

The next morning Ellie and I woke up early and went for a short hike. We climbed the winding trail on a small hill within the Zion Valley and watched the sunrise reflect on the red cliffs. I took a picture of the two of us, rain clouds still in the distance. Ellie told me she might like to do an occasional short day hike but our extended backpacking and climbing treks were now a thing of her past.

For several years before this, Ellie often told me she wanted to hike the Wonderland Trail, a 96-mile circumference of Mount Rainier. This was an extremely popular hike and required reservations months in advance. I worked the system that year and had recently received the confirmation for our 9-day itinerary. It was to be a time for just Ellie and me, hiking a short 8-10 miles per day and letting the natural art inspire some sketches and drawings during the evenings around camp. At the apex of the short hike in Zion, we agreed the Wonderland trail would not see us that summer. I said I was ok with it, but one of my life dreams quietly withered and died.

Looking at the picture of Ellie and I on the hill in Zion National Park, I can see I missed the signs once again. Another change had begun. I can now see it in Ellie's smile. The clouds are starting to clear somewhat above the cliffs in the background and there is a clarity in Ellie's eyes.

Ellie's junior year ended and we took a family vacation to the Redwoods in California. We hit a new vacation low that year. The weather outside the tent was the same as inside our hearts, gloomy with drizzle, little or no hope for a sunny day. The week could not end quickly enough.

Mid-week we met my parents at Crater Lake. The morning after meeting them, Ellie and I ran ten miles up the mountain and back down to our camp. The run up the ancient volcano was a second sign of change. It was a long, tough run, and she stayed with it every step of the way. Ellie was coming back.

When we returned from Oregon and California, Ellie signed up for a houseboat trip with our church youth group. Ann and I were concerned about what could happen, afraid of circumstances that seemed, to us, the worst thing for her. She packed lightly at the last minute and left with the other kids. Ann and I worried about how she would react to the food, the people, but most of all to being trapped on a boat. We thought there would be no refuge, no place to hide from her fears. We were wrong about Ellie's reaction. Ann had been prepared for the houseboat trip by the voice in our kitchen. It was time now and we let go.

Ellie returned from the houseboat trip on Lake Roosevelt, the lake formed by the Grand Coulee Dam in Eastern Washington. She said she found the answers to her fears there. She found her faith was in God and realized that trying to please people would never give her hope. She insisted that she would be ok with food and no longer needed to find hope in the vision she was vainly seeking to create in the mirror. The next day, the recycle bin was filled to over the brim with fashion magazines. Ellie not only sat at the dinner table, she ate with us.

When we look for the answers within ourselves, when we start to believe that we have the powers of God, or are even god ourselves, we lose. Ann received the answer. Ellie's earthly father was not able to fix this one but her heavenly father could. I should have known that and rested easily.

The next winter was not without its challenges. Ellie's dark clouds returned several times but the demons seemed to stay at bay.

As winter turned to spring it was obvious Ellie brokered a tenuous truce with her unseen enemies. Ellie's transformation was not yet complete and the story, which unfolded over the next two years, surprised me even more.

Ellie and I went snowshoeing together the next winter. It was our first hike of the next stage in both of our lives. She enjoyed the woods immensely and said she might want to hike more. I stumbled on to CCC Tree #1 in the Middle Fork Valley, my first old growth giant and the most beautiful tree in the world.

My search for trees was, at the end of 2008, just as poised for something new as Ellie's life when she boarded the houseboat in the summer of 2007. There are two arrows on the sign leading into the Pratt Valley. The "Big Trees" are only one alternative.

# Chapter 7: Big Tree Art

*We walk around like poems---our lives infused with meaning beyond ourselves.*

*(Lyanda Lynn Haupt, <u>Crow Planet</u>, Little-Brown, 2009)*

The North Bend Timber Company left The Pratt Valley in 1941. The rails pulled, the camps removed, everything valuable taken with them. The valley floor was virtually devoid of trees, the tall firs, cedars, and spruces taken to the mill, now at Bryn Mayr, and sawed into lumber for the post-depression growth in a country bursting onto the world stage. For reasons lost to history, a large swath of trees, a grove, was left high in the valley while lower down, without any reasonable expectation, a smaller patch of tall trees remained close to the river's mouth. In the 1960's, the rail grade now a trail, someone made and placed a sign indicating the presence of this old growth stand.

The sign was made with an attempt to match the "Smokey the Bear" colors of the Forest Service in the 1950's and 1960's. A crisp, chocolate brown background with a bright yellow border and letters. The ensuing decades took their toll on the small six by ten inch sign, nailed to the second growth spruce. Wind and weather tore at the underlying cedar board while the Forest Service changed its attitude toward colors, construction, and wilderness signage in general. By the turn of the new millennium, the sign lay literally in shards at the base of the tree but it still served its purpose, pointing hikers towards the old trees. Some anonymous trail guardian had scratched "main trail" and an arrow pointing left to delineate that this was, in fact, a fork in the trail.

I was disappointed to find that sign laying on the ground in tatters when I arrived in late 2008. Motivated in early 2009, I talked my dad out of a nice, thick piece of cedar board and, using my plunge router, made a new sign. The letters were now black, the sign natural, more in line with the Forest Service's newer guidelines. But to actually hang the sign in the forest would be an act of civil disobedience. After camping by the Middle Fork at the Pratt River mouth, Ellie and I packed the sign, an axe with a hammer-head, and three twenty-penny heavy-galvanized nails up the Pratt Valley and replaced the sign.

The sign, placed exactly where the previous one once hung covered an old blaze. The blaze was where a woodsman long ago used an axe to scar the tree and mark the trail. Literally, they "blazed the trail". Layered over that historic trail indicator my sign now gave guidance to anyone who came up the valley. The "Big Trees" were to the right, while the "Main Trail", was to the left.

Pounding three nails into that tree I crossed the line between observing history into being part of it. I was no longer a spectator in this forest; I was playing a bit part in its story.

On the surface, art is a way to speak. In practice art is a perspective. During my last year in the Air Force I started to draw...or perhaps I started to paint. Looking at my attempts at art from that time it is hard to tell what I was doing. My drawings were two-dimensional and lacking life. Some looked like casual architectural drawings. Others appear focused on flowers. All were attempts to find why I wanted to paint or draw.

Preparing to climb Mount Index in 2002, I painted this stunning mountain's North Wall. Staring at the pictures I had taken from various angles, I was forced to consider every detail in order to produce the small drawing. The approach slabs, the bowl, the upper ridge, the false summit, they became 'real' with each brush stroke. My first attempt to actually climb the peak with Paul, who I had so much climbing success with, failed miserably after only four of the 16 required pitches. I went home in self-imposed disgrace and painted a dark, foreboding picture of the mountain. It contained little or no detail.

I set my sites on the North Face of the North Tower of Index with no time frame but a definitive training program. Weekly workouts at the local outdoor climbing wall while wearing a pack with a twenty pound paving brick were interspersed with 'hang-dog' sessions from rafters in our garage. I painted the North Tower in large scale. The smaller details became larger, the steep wall above the slabs, the ramps below the bowl, a small ledge just short of the upper ridge. The first time I was not prepared, mentally or physically, next time I would be ready.

Bradley and I climbed the North Face of Mt. Index's North Tower in 2004. Twenty-eight hours car to car marked the hardest climb I ever attempted and will probably ever do. Late on the first day we were stuck midway up the bowl. Desperately we searched for a small, flat place to sleep for the night, a bivy site. Etched in my mind from the hours I spent creating the painting was the small ledge which should be just above us. We slept fitfully on that coffee-table-sized rock mattress and summitted the next morning. The large painting hangs in my office now, the small shelf that was our bed just visible in mixed media of ink over watercolor pencils.

Art allowed me to "see" a mountain and find a place to sleep.

A friend from work and I once skipped out of a construction equipment trade show in Germany and visited the Munich Art Museum. Mike has a minor in art history in addition to his degree and masters in engineering. He gave me a guided tour of the art. At thirty-five years old, it was my first time in an art museum. Western art followed many of the same patterns as my drawing and painting. Looking at those paintings, I felt my two-dimensional life desperately needed a Renaissance.

I spent the first twenty-eight years of my life ignoring art. Art represented a "weaker way of looking at life" and lacked the pragmatic realism of engineering. I recognized art only as function and nothing else. Like many aspects of the world and life, I dismissed art and filed it neatly away.

I planned for Zach to learn to climb with me, just like Bradley. At ten years old I took Zach on a two-day trip to climb The Queens, north of Lake Kachess just over Snoqualmie Pass. We hiked along the shores of the lake, turned up the Mineral Creek trail, beat through some brush then climbed straight up a steep, forested hill. After attaining the ridge, we slipped through a minor pass and made camp on the heather field next to a miniscule lake. There were no signs of people.

The next morning, Zach and I strapped on our climbing gear and crossed the snowfields. We roped up below the cliffs and started the easy scramble on an exposed ridge to the summit. Zach climbed only a few feet and froze. He didn't want to climb. This was not my plan, but this was my son.

The incident on The Queens was a strange precursor to Zach's and my expedition into the Pratt four years later. The little sketch of the u-bolt stakeholder intrigued both of us and the picture taken by Darius Kinsey firmly tied that relic to the logging history of the Middle Fork Valley. Returning home, I dug out the copies I made of the <u>Pratt River Logging Camp Evaluation</u>, rereading it this time with more care and interest. The social history was intriguing. The economic uncertainty that swept the globe in late 2008 made stories of Robert Vinnedge in the Great Depression much more personal than I anticipated.

I contacted the Snoqualmie Valley Historical Society again. I hoped to arrange to use some of their historic photographs on my middleforkgiants website. My first meeting was with the person with authority to approve using the photos. An appointment was arranged with the Snoqualmie Valley Historical Society Board President, Gardiner Vinnedge, none other than the grandson of the owner of the North Bend Timber Company.

The Snoqualmie Valley Museum is nothing spectacular to look at from outside, and is somewhat undeveloped inside. Gardiner asked to meet at 10:00 on a Saturday morning and, sitting in my truck at 10:15 on this cold December day, it seemed odd that he was not here fifteen minutes late. Finally I took a walk around the back, found the door ajar and stepped in to meet a tall gentleman in his fifties who introduced himself simply as "Gardiner" and pulled two old wooden chairs into the middle of the main exhibit area. He offered one to me.

Gardiner gave a very brief overview of the Snoqualmie Valley's history and his involvement with the museum, bringing together the historical stories, and some of the struggles involved in preserving them. He knew a little about The Middle Fork but repeatedly deferred to Dick Kirby's first-hand knowledge. I was impressed by Gardiner's humble, yet knowledgeable presence. I hoped I would have some opportunity to work with him in the future. Like Dick, Gardiner was a teacher.

January 2009 was my month to write the cover story for The Platform, our company newspaper. I wanted to do something other than the typical "executive blather" piece. Orders for our construction equipment had come to a crashing halt in the previous three months. Layoffs left many of my coworkers without jobs and there was a dark vacancy to the empty corridors in the office building where I worked. With almost no capital available, plans to expand our production across three continents slowed almost to a halt. It was hauntingly like the situation R.W. Vinnedge faced with his 1929 plan to expand logging operations into the Pratt Valley.

Gardiner worked with me in writing an article about his grandfather's challenges in the early 1930s. Like us, Robert Vinnedge was forced to shut down portions of his business and lay off his logging teams. A notebook of personal letters from the elder Mr. Vinnedge was insightful to understand the man who was part of the Middle Fork's history. The article took shape as a comparison of two struggles, personal, financial, trying, separated by seventy years.

R.W. Vinnedge's struggle, expressed in his letters, spoke directly to me. In January 1932, Vinnedge wrote, "There is no improvement in the lumber market yet. I feel this year will be some better than last but I do not expect to show any great amount of excess prosperity. ...There are too many fundamental things wrong yet to permit of normal conditions." I could write the same thing about the construction equipment market and the business I was in. A person from the Middle Fork's past seemed to be talking directly to me.

Gardiner made several references during our two-hour talk about the lack of historical information on the Middle Fork. He said they were trying to convince Dick Kirby to write a book about it but Dick had other commitments. Gardiner was hopeful for a historical project of some sort.

Unlike the search for the largest tree, a reprise of the hunts repeated by other people such as Richard Preston (author of Wild Trees), the search for history in the Middle Fork was largely unprecedented. The human story of the Valley needed someone to paint its portrait. At first it seemed the website would be the way to do that. The intrigue I felt years ago over the Holder Creek Train wreck, showed to me on Tiger Mountain by Bill Longwell, re-ignited.

The week after Christmas 2008 was marked in Western Washington by harsh rains and floods. Trapped indoors, blocked from going into the Valley, Zach and I spent time watching movies and talking. Zach enjoyed skateboarding, he practiced over many months to the point that he exhibited some pretty skillful displays at the skate park, on the streets, or in our driveway. At first I was skeptical of his skateboarding, a "slacker activity", it hardly qualified as a noble pursuit. With time I became more impressed.

Zach enjoyed taking videos of he and his friends' skate antics, editing them together, and posting them on the web. Although there are literally thousands of these sorts of videos on the popular, user-uploaded video sites, Zach's seemed to stand out for their artistic and unique approach. He received a number of comments from unknown amateur critics complimenting him on film technique. There was a hint to a decent skater with a gift for capturing art on video.

Inspired by his video success and tied with a drive to accomplish something, far from the "slacker" approach, Zach was taking video courses in school and was showing a growing interest in film as a life interest. Ann and I gave him a nicer video camera for Christmas and he was making creative use of it. His online picture was a self-portrait with his camera.

As often happens in life, a half dozen seemingly unrelated aspects came together during the New Year 2009 week. Inspired, Zach and I decided the way to "see" the Middle Fork history was to film it. My type-A, goal-driven quest for the largest tree had come to a fork in the trail and there was a choice. I chose to steer away from my big trees and pursue art instead. Big Tree Art.

## Have you seen the Bicycle Riding Goat?

In 2006, with the sun tucked behind sandstone walls, Ann and I sat on the banks of a dirty little river looking up at the cliffs towering above us. Named Turkey Pen ruin by those who found it 800 years after its inhabitants had abandoned the area, the tiny cliff dwelling sat improbably perched on a shelf that, from below, looked more imagined than real. It was our first night in Grand Gulch, having descended during the day from the rim, and the trailhead, above. Once again, the Allen family was in the deserts of southern Utah.

I enjoyed the opportunity to be overnighting in the wilderness with Ann. Although we packed in a couple of times when first married twenty years ago, we had only backpacked once since. Our three kids were a half-mile upstream at our tiny camp, hidden behind small cottonwoods on an almost manicured looking lawn.

I worked quickly to sketch the little ruin. This was the ostensive reason for our evening trip. The sketch was not going well, not being a natural artist, I tend to do better when sketching frequently and subjects I am more familiar with. I couldn't remember my last sketch and this was far different than the evergreen forests and mountains of the Pacific Northwest.

We had seen only two other people so far in Grand Gulch. Volunteer rangers, they checked our required permit, ubiquitous reminders we were on federal land. We were startled by the noise when an unidentified man pushed through the brush along the trail from down stream and approached us.

"Have you seen our friend?" Wearing only shorts and a hydration-type backpack, he was sun burnt, unshaven, dirty, and obviously tired. He was covered with sweat dripping down his bare skin. He asked about his other companion urgently, but in the friendly 'can't seem to find him but he's around here somewhere' sort of way.

I was just ready to say I had not seen anyone when he blurted out "HE'S LOOKING FOR THE BICYCLE RIDING GOAT!"

It suddenly seemed much later in the evening, darker in this secluded little canyon. I was confused.

There are times that something is put into your head that turns everything else sideways. Just like the spinning hourglass in a Windows operating system, my mind was processing and nothing was coming out.

Dumb look from me. Blank stare from Ann. Urgent inquisitive expression from our new friend. Another hiker now stood behind him. In retrospect I'm not sure I could describe any differences between them. Looking back, I'm pretty sure there were two, they just looked alike. Maybe there was only one.

"Well, perhaps you have seen the bicycle riding goat? We're looking for the bicycle riding goat. Have you seen it?" He stopped. His questions visibly begged for explanations on every level.

My stare transitioned to a mesmerized look. All I could eak out was "No". The searchers of billy the cyclist ran on upstream. We never saw them again, nor did we ever see their friend.

But what about the goat? What could a bicycle riding goat be? Was it just going to ride by? Was it some mysterious type of mammal? A hiking moniker? The secret of all truth? A haven of rest for the weary soul? A wise person in the wilderness? An apparition who provides for eternal bliss? The bicycle riding goat.

I stared at Ann, she stared at me.

The next day the five of us, Bradley, Ellie, Zach, Ann, and I, took off on a day-hike downstream to visit the various sites of the ancient Anasazi civilization. We told the kids the story of the two explorers, their missing friend and the goat. Somehow they had not heard them go by the camp. Interesting? No way out of this canyon except upstream or down, where had the goat-searchers gone?

Small ruins sat at the bases of red, sandstone cliffs. Others were, like Turkey Pen, often up high, defenses against long-gone enemies. Not formally marked, we followed way trails and marks to south-facing alcoves in the red-rock walls. Rock art, petroglyphs and pictographs adorned the cliffs while the refuse of daily life centuries ago littered the ground below each brick building. Midden piles full of corn cobs, pottery shards, and other detritus of history lay in front of each ancient doorway.

One small path snaked through some trees, up a brush filled slope to an overhanging wall. Few buildings stood within this ruin but there were certainly signs of life. Rock art adorned the walls, many high up where the artist had stood on long ago roofs and walls to leave their mark.

What motivates these pictures? Museum and park tours will talk about spiritual motives, cultural traditions, and messages to related groups. Somehow I see an individual with some passion and a need to express. Ancient graffiti. Some as simple as hand prints traced on the rock. Some as sophisticated as...

I laughed out loud. I laughed some more. I was suddenly very pleased with the whole trip. I had found the highlight of this spring break. I called for Ann and the kids to come up because everyone should, at some point in their life, view.....


......the Bicycle Riding Goat.

The economy was no better, it was mostly worse. One of Robert Vinnedge's letters came to me, seemingly just as poignant now as it was in 1932, "I have arrived at the point where I don't worry myself sick over it as I used to. It does no good and furthermore makes one a curse to both himself and his family." I would not be a curse. Zach and I needed to make art, we needed to "see" the Valley.

The hunt for big trees morphed during this renaissance, no longer a goal-oriented quest with fame and glory as the carrot, this was now a journey to be lived. History is people and just like the Pratt Logging Camp study, the real archeology lay not in the ground but with the people who created the story.

To make our film, Zach and I required support from the historical society. We needed help applying for a grant but, even more importantly, needed permission to use their historical photographs. Working together, he and I prepared a presentation for their board.

The eight members of the board sat in a semi-circle while Zach and I stood in front of them. I would present, then turn it over to Zach. He clearly presented how we would tell the Middle Fork story and explained the technical aspects of the film project. One slide showed the ruins of the Taylor Ranger Station. Dick Kirby, sitting with the other board members, told us about working there. History had a face.

My fourteen-year-old son was a convincing presence, even deftly answering some of their questions. We received the Snoqualmie Valley Historical Society's support.

Project Sand Shed, code name for our film project, was my bicycle-riding goat for 2009. Named after a historical ruin in the Valley, it was a serendipitous pursuit sprung up from the red-rock walls of life and presented both a distraction as well as yet another aspect of transformation.

Looking back, I should have seen it coming. Like the bicycle riding goat in Grand Gulch, there were telltale signs of more to this Middle Fork forest than just trees.

## Tracks

| Number of Toes | Claws | General Shape | General Outline | Family |
|---|---|---|---|---|
| 2 | Dew claws | | | Deer |
| 4 | Yes | | | Dog |
| 4 | No | | | Cat |
| 4 | Rarely | | | Rabbit |
| 5* | Sometimes | | | Bear |
| 5* | Sometimes | | | Weasel |
| 5 | Sometimes | | | Raccoon |

F = Front,   H = Hind
*fifth toe may not show

## Scat

| Shape | Number | General Outline | Family |
|---|---|---|---|
| long sphere | clumps, groups | | Deer |
| thick cord | single, several | | Dog |
| broken cord | single | | Cat |
| sphere | few, scattered | | Rabbit |
| thick cords | single, piles | | Bear |
| looped cords | single | | Weasel |
| thick cords | single, piles | | Raccoon |

# Chapter 8: Jeep Girl

*I desire the circumstance,*

*to choose to live or die.*

*The best description of my place is*

*Beyond the trail am I*

composed in 2007
in the Bailey Range

They had first aid kits, yes, and stretchers. But, anybody seriously hurt…you were looking at….at the least, an hour and a half. Like in the upper Middle Fork or Pratt River. You were looking at least an hour and a half before you could get medical attention.

And why Howard didn't die, I'll never know.

Well, the only reason he didn't bleed to death is this log just pinched his leg so bad…it was cut off. It was. But it sealed it, you know, he didn't bleed that bad. And we bound it up, you know, with shirts and under shirts. And we had to pack him… it was about two thousand feet.

That's when we had to pack him down to the railroad track. And then the speeder was gone. We had to haul him to Camp Brown on a railroad car with a 'loci'. He was about…that man was two and a half hours before he….they met him with an ambulance at Camp 15.

The Hospital was down here in Snoqualmie Falls."

*Herb Ray (logger in the Middle Fork and Pratt Valleys during the 1930's in a 1989 taped interview for the U.S. Forest Service)*

Ask someone what a tree is made of, if there were a recipe for trees what would be the ingredients? A typical answer would be "dirt" and a few might add, "Water". Barely half true, the answer is much more simple and elegant. If trees were actually made of dirt, then a large tree would have a hole around it, the bowl from which the dirt was removed to make the tree. The simplistically beautiful truth is trees are made almost exclusively of water and carbon dioxide. Useless to us, this waste from our breath, the air devoid of oxygen that we would suffocate in, is the forest's buffet.

Chemistry provides the basic equation for trees. Take water, $H_2O$, combine with our breath, $CO_2$, add some energy provided by the sun and the product is cellulose, a complex molecule of many forms but literally cooked up from the basic ingredients of Carbon, Hydrogen, and Oxygen. A lengthy word like photosynthesis detracts from this beautiful process.

Photosynthesis in trees is the transformation that defines our world.

There is remarkable beauty in the Pacific Northwest and the forests are a key aspect of it. When I was a kid the vistas were marred by clearcuts, frequently as far as the eye could see. With time, those same areas have now grown back into forests. Replanting and quick re-growth is the happy story told by the forest service and the large, modern lumber companies. But these forests of hybridized Douglas firs are homogeneous and sterile in almost all aspects. A walk under their canopy shows the skinny trunks of a thousand clones, a wheat farm with hundred foot-tall stalks.

There are places where just the right conditions have brought a rebirth of the old growth forests. The right combination of less than perfect clear cutting, little disturbance by man, steep slopes left untouched so the existing trees can prevent erosion, and massive amounts of rain can result in a much more mature and diverse forest.

A true old growth forest takes centuries to develop. It is more than just old trees, it is a community of mosses, lichens, a variety of trees, and plants of many kinds. Deep moss carpets run for miles, fungus of every shape, size and color, grow from everything. Massive fallen trees provide nutrients for new growth. The sun rarely touches the forest floor. Animal populations are sparse and may only live high within the trees' limbs. Old growth is a beauty that is usually only appreciated after seeing it in person.

The Pratt Valley provided just the right combination of elements, watered by 100 inches or more of rain each year. In only seventy years the Douglas firs had naturally grown to heights extending above 150 feet. The few old growth trees are now hard to pick out from their grandchildren. Only their massive trunks give them away. Leafy lichens grow amongst the old timer's and new comer's branches, to fall in a stiff wind and fertilize the rich floor. "Moss grows even on the weeds".

The clearcut is transformed by rain and time.

When Ellie graduated from high school, there was lunch at church for the graduates and their parents. The program contained many of the standard features, a slide show, speeches, and some music. At the end, each graduating senior could go forward with their parents and say something. Ellie told the story about the time I shaved at a campground in Colorado wearing just my underwear. She said at that point she realized how different her dad was and that he really just didn't care what people thought about him. That wasn't completely true but it was something she identified with.

When my time came, I made some comments about the tough times Ellie, Ann, and I went through over the past couple of years. I said several things but started with the story about being in the tent together on Rainier four years prior. When I told the attended group about the fear we shared in that tent I realized *that* fear was more than just for the climb. We feared a coming storm we were all unprepared for. Emotions welled up and I couldn't continue. I walked off the stage in tears.

I truly did not know where things stood. I had a shallow faith in the good that was coming of this situation but wrestled for reassurance. The coming months would provide a number of surprises.

One of the big surprises for us all, during the previous summer, was when Ellie organized and led a backpack trip for a group of church friends. I hoped she might return to enjoying the out of doors but was resigned to her simply looking to do some things with friends. Upon returning, she asked to join a group that I was organizing to climb Mount Rainier the next year.

In all honesty, I put her on the list to climb and included her in the initial meetings just to avoid a conflict I knew would occur when I said "no". I was planning on her either opting out or that I would have to tell her she couldn't go. That is always a tough call. On a couple of occasions I have told people they are not prepared and they can't go. I do not like it and it usually has a permanent affect on our relationship. I definitely didn't want that with Ellie.

As the year progressed, Ellie trained for Rainier with what I assessed as mixed enthusiasm. One hike she would be on top of her game; laughing, excited, running up the trail. The next she would ask to turn back, the request appearing to me to be irregardless of the group's wishes. I was not confident in the result and my private list of who I thought would actually climb didn't include her.

Looking back, as the winter progressed she changed. Increasingly she motivated herself to train. When she missed some key skills training she arranged to make them up. I was still extremely concerned that she would get to the hard parts of the climb and simply want to go back. I anticipated fears creeping in she knew were there but hoped would not materialize. I knew those fears well. I, of course, share them.

Ellie was still training hard in late July. I would learn later that Ellie had a renewed confidence that year and had not shared my fears this time.

Climbing The Mountain in 2008 stands out distinctly from my other climbs. Twenty interested people were whittled down to a twelve-person team. It was longer than previous climbs and required different leadership and logistics. I asked Bradley, now living in a house at college, to help with training and leading the group. The man was different from the boy I had known.

We camped the first night at Glacier Basin. Tucked in a cirque where the forest abruptly transitions to alpine tundra, the large group spread out and prepared for the technical climbing the next day. Bradley had a "presence" now and he coached the rest of the team all evening. We had seven new climbers. Ellie tented with me and showed a remarkably positive attitude that was becoming her trademark. I was busy showing people how to use stoves, tie knots, and watching over some of the weaker team members.

The next day we roped up on the somewhat benign Inter-Glacier. The team required three ropes of four people each. For the first time I was not on the same rope as either Bradley or Ellie. It was different, very different, to see the two of them on the ice but knowing in a fall my actions would have no chance to help them.

Dropping off the Inter-Glacier at a vacant Camp Curtis we entered the much more challenging realm of the Emmons. This glacier was cracked and crevassed. Travel was challenging and at times scary. Far in the distance I saw Bradley carefully test the edges of gaping hundred-foot deep crevasses then jump them. The Lead Dog was on the lead rope and blazing the path. I was at the rear. He didn't seem to hesitate and the teams behind followed in his tracks.

We camped mid-way up the Emmons glacier and opted for a true "alpine start" at midnight. Nourished with some homemade oatmeal bars, we climbed with no moon to light the way. Mid August brought the Perseids meteor shower, falling stars crossing the sky from horizon to horizon gave welcome relief from the unknown glacial terrain. Leading was tough. Compounding this was an icefall that had, at glacial pace, moved across the standard route in the two years since we climbed this route last. Talking with climbing teams coming down the previous day we learned that most were not able to pass through this relatively new challenge.

Bradley led confidently throughout the night. I was pleased he called me up by walkie-talkie at one point to consult my opinion. I agreed with his judgment. All he needed was reassurance.

As Bradley led us through the icefall on The Emmons Glacier's "Corridor", Ellie and I climbed two ropes back. Ellie was the third climber on the second rope; I was the first climber on the third rope. We were close together on the steep ice in the pitch black of midnight and spoke frequently. There were striking differences in our relationship now that she was on another rope.

Ellie obviously was much more comfortable this year in the tent than she was four years before. She joked around. Her voice was excited as she settled into her sleeping bag, less than an inch off the glacial ice. I think she felt the typical fear we average mortals feel when we climb. I feel them on every climb but rarely see them on Bradley's face.

It was still deeply dark at one a.m. when we traversed an angled serac in the ice fall. A house-sized block of ice sat at a steep angle, its slick 'roof' requiring we traverse to pass.

In front of Ellie, on the second rope, was Reid Olson, Ellie's high school youth director and first time climber. Halfway across the serac he lost traction and instantly started sliding down the block. Thirty feet from where Reid's crampons and ice axe came loose from the ice was a crevasse, a hundred foot deep crack into the glacial void. Ellie dug in and her headlamp pointed into Reid's terrified face. Reid stopped his slide, he "arrested" before he went over the edge. I thought Ellie was ready to catch him, but she insisted she was not. It bothered her that she was not ready.

Reid did exactly as he had been trained, laying on his ice axe he dug into the life-saving self-arrest. As Bruce, rope team leader for Ellie's and Reid's rope, belayed his team off the serac it settled into all of us how closely we just came to disaster. Ellie looked at me and said, "I am more scared than I have ever been in my life."

Yet, looking in her eyes, I could see the fear was a different beast. No longer the incapacitating monster that had stalked her for three years, this was the adrenaline-driving fear that motivates action, one I know well and cherish. Ellie dug in and climbed tirelessly for the remaining six hours to the top of Mount Rainier.

Along the summit crater's conical flank, Ellie's character literally beamed. Her rope team was completely bonked, a term used by athletes to describe the state of exhaustion so complete that the body just starts to wilt. The leader was on one knee, interestingly enough he didn't recall that later, the other two members obviously dazed and tired beyond their expectations. As I approached, catching up with my rope team after a slight problem, Ellie looked casual and waved to me.

On the summit, Ellie was jovial and kidded around for our pictures. Ellie clearly showed the demeanor of a climber who had summitted before. Cool and casual, she walked around and enjoyed the view.

Late that afternoon, I was the last person to walk into the Emmons Flats Glacier Camp, the rest of the team was already sprawled on the ice trying to unstick boots from bloody socks and ooze themselves into bags desperate for exhausted slumber. Bradley stood in the middle, casual, as if nothing much had happened. Everyone was pleased with the day both for reaching the summit and returning safely.

One person asked me my secret for leadership. "Simple, I put the best man in front and lead quietly from the rear." The Army is getting my best man.

Returning to Rainier seemed to confirm something deep inside Ellie. She hiked more, talked about life in a much more carefree way, and relished driving the jeep she bought a month before. Her jeep quickly took on the personality of the new Ellie, stickers started to show up on the back; "Got Oxygen?", a peace sign, or one that just says the word "Hike".

At first, her jeep brought on a new found freedom and the desire to strike out alone. One weekend she decided to drive up the Middle Fork and camp by herself. Late that evening, she came back home, not quite ready to sleep in the woods solo. I do not blame her, I have only slept alone a couple of times and it is scary. The warmth, light breathing, or just the knowledge of someone nearby is pure gold.

Ellie read <u>Into the Wild,</u> the story of Chris McCandles who takes off solo on a soul-searching path that eventually leads to Alaska. In the wilds of frozen Alaska he dies alone in an abandoned bus. The story is captivating. I feel the call to roam every time I read it. Ellie feels the same pull and wants to do some traveling. It's a healthy tension in a young heart with some searching still to do.

Ellie and I returned together to the Middle Fork Valley during February of 2009. Using a canoe, we crossed the river and camped in a small grove of large spruce trees by the mouth of the Pratt River. The Pratt Valley sprawled behind us, its deep forests beckoning our sojourn the next day, but after a short exploratory hike in the evening, we decided to make a fire.

The gray skies became more damp as the evening went on, a drop, a sprinkle, enough to motivate us to pull our raincoats out but never enough to actually call "rain". We walked northeast along the old logging road then came back along the river looking for the sites where cabins once stood. There were no signs; time, moisture, forest, and a wandering river had erased them. Sitting under the tall spruce by our tent, there was a more determined pattern to the moisture coming from the sky.

Ellie and I collected some dry wood and sticks. An old growth hollow stump provided a sheltered kiln for decaying cedar to dehydrate. I pulled large, red blocks of the fine-grained wood out and split it into kindling. Ellie was surprised that I brought an axe with us.

Pulling one of the dry bags from the pile beside the tent, I rummaged around until the food bag finally fell to the forest floor. Picking it up, I "unzipped" the plastic bag and pulled two small sheets of newspaper out, packed just for this occasion. Ellie asked how I remembered all of the things to bring, it seemed like we always had what we needed.

Crumpled up newspaper, then some small, dry sticks, and finally some shaved cedar provided a foundation for a little teepee of wood. Some more wood went on top. As the drips from the ink-dark sky turned to a slight drizzle, we put match to paper and nothing happened.....Oh, it crackled, a flame lit, there were sparks but eventually the paper sort of "embered away" and the twigs, shavings, and wood lay unscathed. How did anyone ever manage to start a forest fire out here?

"I'm not your Grandpa Allen", I told Ellie. Dad would have had a fire going by now; blazing, cheerful, warm. He might have, like he often did, taken a single match from his little silver waterproof container, screwed the lid back on and packed the rest of the matches away only to say "a real woodsman only needs a single match to start a fire". Whoever I am, I don't seem to be a real woodsman and still strive, in some ways, to match the standard Dad set.

It took two more tries but Ellie and I eventually started a fire. The drizzle became a sprinkle and, for a while, it rained. We were warm under our giant spruce and the fire entertained us that night. Later, after throwing the fire, bit by bit, into the river, we climbed into the tent and Ellie fell blissfully, peacefully, asleep. Seemingly, all of her fears were gone.

There is a fourth message on the back of Ellie's jeep, a small rectangular sticker, it reads, "Think Globally, Act Locally".

Ellie feels a call to serve. Ellie's story is my story in many ways. There are aspects of that story I wish I didn't share, like paralyzing fears. There are aspects I am pleased she has, like the need to serve others. And there are aspects that translate as pure joy, like standing on Mount Rainier for the second time.

There is a joy to life that, much like the elegantly beautiful act of a growing tree, is just too profound to put to words.

# Chapter 9: Red Rocks

*My love affair with trees is not monogamous. I love rocks too.*

Middle Fork history certainly did not start with the North Bend Timber Company, the first prospectors, or even the Snoqualmie Indians. Carved and shaped, it reflects geological forces and the cumulative affects of small changes over eons.

Mount Garfield, towering over the confluence of the Middle Fork and Taylor Rivers, marks the meeting of three distinct geological formation types. Igneous intrusions (lava which has cooled underground) meet layered sedimentary rock from ancient islands that long ago combined with the North American mainland. Volcanic igneous rock prominently fills the third formational group, ridges that emanate from Mt. Garfield . When the igneous intrusions flowed in molten form against the other rocks, spaces formed, minute holes and cracks. For millions of years superheated steam, saturated with copper, quartz, and other valuable minerals, flowed through these cracks leaving rich deposits.

Once formed, the rock formations and mountains in the Middle Fork were worked by glaciers and eroded by water. The distinctive u-shaped valley is a telltale sign of glacial carving. The remnants of these mighty ice sheets still cling to Mount Hinman at the river's headwaters.

During the last ice age, which ended about 10,000 years ago, glaciers in the Puget Sound basin stretched south of Seattle and dammed the flow of water from the Cascade Mountains. Giant lakes filled and drained, quickly shaping the land as ice dams formed then melted and broke.

Most of this ancient geological history lies below topsoil and forest clinging to the steep valley walls. Where rocks do protrude, lush moss covers them in acre-wide carpets. The Middle Fork's geology, below the alpine zone, is cloaked by forest.

Ultimately I needed to face the reasons I went to the Middle Fork. I went there to escape. Escape the stresses of a new role at work that I was struggling to come to terms with. Escape from a worldwide recession that seemed to have more stress than pain. Escape from my role in downsizing the very jobs and people I firmly believed were "the sheep" Dave Mock talked about me caring for.

It was time to walk out of the valley and find the mission I knew I was called to pursue. Where were the sheep who need to be fed? There was one place I knew I could depend on for answers. For perspective I left the Middle Fork Valley and headed for the red rocks in the Desert Southwest.

**P**oor in Spirit: When I walked in to Reverend Dave Mock's parish I had a story. For me, this story was the standard by which I measured the world.

I was supremely confident I could explain not only the situation others were in but how they could positively escape their predicaments with the same success with which I avoided them. I created a world-order of meritocracy where I uniquely deserved everything I had.

Ellie once came home with a new phrase, learned from her teacher at school, she was certain I would not know the meaning of. She said I possessed an "excess of certitude". Naturally, I knew exactly what she meant.

The desert is a special place, a stark contrast to the lush forests and moss-carpeted valleys of the Pacific Northwest. We have travelled several times to southern Utah and northern Arizona in the eight years since Ann first convinced me to go south. Captivated by the narrow canyons, dry washes, green oasis, and isolated towns, I immersed myself in the writings of Edward Abbey, John Wesley Powell, and Everett Ruess.

Of our eight trips to the Southwest, two stand out. In 2004 we drove, hiked, wandered, and tent-camped for three full weeks. The family together for 23 straight days, we bonded in a timeless way. For the second, in 2007, it was only Zach and me. I told him we were going to spend the whole week in southern Utah during spring break. We would live out of the truck and wouldn't pay for anyplace to camp. I filled the then nearly new Nissan Frontier with camping gear, backpacks, lots of food, and my Dutch oven. It was our "dirt-bagging" trip.

I picked Zach up after school on a Thursday and we drove southeast through Oregon into Idaho. It got late east of Boise and I felt too tired to drive. Pulling over onto an isolated farm road at 11:00 PM, we threw a tarp down and went to sleep. Zach said, "Dad, I told my friends we were sleeping on the side of the road but thought it was just an expression". At 1:30 a.m. we met the local sheriff. Nice man, he was making sure we were alive.

We continued into Utah, drove ever further south, kicked up dust along the Old Sheffield Road and pitched our tent in a wide spot, a distinctive red-rock outcrop only yards from our little camp. After a rich dinner made with bacon and Bisquick baked to perfection in my cast-iron oven, we lay down in the tent as the sun went down. Zach read from Into the Wild while I read The Monkey Wrench Gang. Krakauer and Abbey, what a pair.

Those who mourn: In Wild at Heart, a book on dealing with life as an upper middle-class man with no real problems but acting like there are, is an intriguing quote. It is attributed to a secondary source and reads:

*"Don't ask yourself what the world needs. Ask yourself what makes you come alive, because what the world needs is people who have come alive."*

These words spoke directly to me so I researched the original author. They were from a book written by Howard Thurman. I searched out and read the stories of this preacher and philosopher.

Born in 1899, Howard Thurman was raised in a house where his grandmother lived. She was born a slave. Howard Thurman went on to become Reverend Thurman and wrote several books. One book he wrote in 1949, <u>Jesus and the Disinherited</u> is rumored to be the only book, other than the Bible, Martin Luther King Jr. carried with him at all times.

I was not acquainted with the disinherited.

Zach was thirteen years old and things were hot and cold between us. Zach is like me in many ways. He enjoys things that are on the edges of popular, often finding his own "cool". He is creative, and at that time he was making T-shirts. He even developed his own brand name: Plaid.

But Zach is also ever bit as determined, stubborn and 'certain' as I am. We regularly argued. Frequently small things, a homework problem or some bit of household discipline, flare into a major confrontation.

Ann and I talked frequently about it and she was convinced I was permanently alienating Zach. He was certainly different than Bradley or Ellie, liking different things and showing his passions in a very visible way. Yet, he was neither rebellious nor vindictive. It bothered me that he was frequently disrespectful and, in my mind, I feared this was developing into open rebellion.

Zach was not interested in hiking in the mountains, possibly a conscious contrast to Bradley and the validity Bradley found through climbing. Zach and I kayaked together, it helped, but we were not bonding. The trip to Utah was definitely a risk. Ann and I were both concerned that Zach and I would simply argue, bicker, and grump at each other for an entire week.

**Meek:** There is no control for the disinherited. The world spins around at a pace and manner that they have no control over and never will. Others, those in power, not only control this spin, the control is absolute. The sun for the disinherited rises and sets on the commands of the wealthy. Darkness of night, light of day, their life's story is written on the whims of others. Hope is not something they have lost, it is a void they were born without. They have no inheritance in this world. The disinherited.

Integrating Howard Thurman's writing, several articles on helping the poor as well as the book <u>Walking with the Poor</u> by Bryant Myers I concluded there are three key attributes common to those who are disinherited:

1.    Belief that you have no say in life's direction.

2.      Belief that others have absolute say over their own lives as well as yours

3.      A life of damaged and dysfunctional relationships. Those who should provide healthy leadership in life; employers, government, churches, and even God, are using you for their ends or absent.

I tried to imagine living life in this framework? Nothing to build on, nothing to grow, no earth to cultivate seed in. Life is merely endured.

Redefining the concept of being poor as being "disinherited" from society instead defining it as a lack of resources; food, water, shelter, was stunning. Howard Thurman's writing changed me. Previously the poor, destitute and unworthy were enough for my charity. Now my view opened up and I broadened the definition of who needed to be listened to. Not only is the world full of people who are disinherited but I realized only giving them 'stuff' does little or nothing to help them develop the relationships they starve for.

Zach and I descended into the canyons the second day. That was why we were there and I was chomping at the bit to go. Twelve miles of cross-country desert with two slot canyons was our "practice day". We were confident and ready for more.

Six miles in we walked side-by-side through Harris wash. Zach said to me "Dad, some kids asked if the hiking in the desert meant we would be finding dead cow skulls and stuff." We both laughed.

We walked around the bend to a long, straight stretch, the wash now almost a quarter-mile wide. A small white dot glinted in the sun on a grass-covered rise in front of us. As we got closer we both realized what it was...a sun-bleached cow skull. The desert was as bleak as Zach's friends envisioned. We were enjoying every minute.

I realized how well Zach and I were getting along.

**H**unger and Thirst for Righteousness: At Christmas Ann, Zach, and I helped with a dinner party for women and children from various shelters around the city. We men were asked to simply serve. Humbly we were to exemplify the role of servant. We did it with pleasure. "Yes ma'am, would you care for some more coffee".

After dinner one of the table hosts told us about a lady at her table who never once in her life, until that day, had been served a cup of coffee by another person, let alone a man. I realized how I take for granted the hundreds of times I am served.

I began to understand that I must approach people in a manner that allowed me to listen to what they said. Sitting in an office, a suburban house, a chain coffee shop, there is no hope of hearing, let alone listening and understanding. A simple Jewish carpenter fulfilled those who lacked the relationships required in life, no crown required.

What does it feel like to believe you are not worthy to be served?

Shortly after leaving our kitschy symbol of desert austerity, Zach and I sat down in a cliff's shade to escape the rising desert spring heat. I was just starting to sweat and felt a little hungry. Our practice-hike was perfect, no one in sight, not even a track. Across Harris Wash was a rock outcrop; layers of red and brown were slightly tilted to the horizontal. I pulled my sketchpad from my pack and started to draw. I thought back to my hike into the Grand Canyon five years before.

In 2001, Bradley and I hiked to the Colorado River from the South Rim of the Grand Canyon and back in a day. It was New Years day. We started before dawn on an ice-covered trail and were back at the hotel by late afternoon. I was struck by the rock layers as we descended the South Kaibab trail.

Neatly the Grand Canyon's horizontal layers marched me through time as I descended the trail. Chinle, Moenkopi, Kaibab, Toroweap, Coconino, Hermit, Supai, Redwall Limestone (my favorite), Muav, Bright Angel, Tapeats. It was as new, beautiful and brilliant as it must have been to John Wesley Powell when he saw it in 1869 during his first descent of the Colorado River. All of this fit neatly into the construct I grew up with.

I think as I am conditioned to think. A strong Evangelical Calvinist Protestant upbringing with a firm overlay of Western logical literalism and a bolster of American-centric Biblical interpretation. This left me with a young earth to look at and a host of nice explanations for what, at first, might appear to be 150 million years of geologic progression. I was confident the geology around me was the result of lesser forces enacted over a few thousand years.

Then I descended to the Grand Canyon Super Group. My universal construct collapsed from the intellectual weight of an ancient mountain range's 20-degree tilt, the millions of years of erosion to flat, and the earth-movement as that range sunk into the Visnu Schyst of the Basement Rocks.

I felt helpless denying what I saw to live securely in an unsupported construct. Thoughts of desert sediment, lost continents, fossilized creatures, and the origins of our world swirled in my mind.

I was disappointed with my drawing.

**M**erciful: My parents started me early on "doing the right thing". I focused on doing no wrong and felt good when I succeeded. I accepted society's definition of the best as simply avoiding the worst. Life was guided by lists of rules; codes of ethics, human resource manuals, and Sunday morning sermons. Why is it common to see the Ten Commandments carved on a wall but rare to see the quote from the book of James: "He who knows the good he should do and doesn't do it, sins"?

I was coming to realize I needed to take on the burdens of those who struggle to carry them. The more my eyes opened, the more I saw the burdens others carried.

Two strange series of events in 2006 led me in a direction I didn't suspect, let alone anticipate. In the first I overheard two colleagues discussing a trip to Nicaragua with a development group called Agros. Phil was seeking financial support to join a group visiting poor people in Nicaragua. I barged into the conversation and offered to contribute. When Phil returned from Central America a few weeks later, he proposed a plan to organize a more ambitious group in Redmond to support a village in rural, Spanish-speaking Nicaragua. It was a bold plan. I listened.

Later that month an old friend, whom I had not seen in over fourteen years, called me from a local jail and asked me to visit him. Sitting in the waiting room, the visiting families mostly spoke Spanish.

I bought a Spanish-language Bible and some language training software. I felt called to learn to speak Spanish.

After a short detour into the haunting beauty in Zebra Slot, its photogenic walls a mere shoulder's width apart, its red stripes tightly spaced and intense, Zach and I left Harris wash. Working our way up a shallow, unnamed wash we came across iron nodules scattered across the red sandstone. These almost uniform brown spheres are hard on the outside but only slightly consolidated sand within. They form inside the sandstone, are visible in the walls of Zebra slot, and eroded out to lie on the surface at our feet.

Harder and more resilient than the surrounding sandstone, eons of erosion leave the ground strewn with the little balls. They are not well understood and still present a geological mystery. I started to contemplate how long it would take for these thousands of balls to come out of the sandstone and roll to the little depression we stood in but was interrupted by Zach. His and my conversation digressed.

This was our first time to encounter nodules and Zach speculated. "I am pretty sure aliens caused this," he said.

Zach frequently sees the signs of alien life. This did not displease me because it meant on day three of our wilderness dirt-bagging excursion we transcended into the trifecta of hiking philosophy: God, Quantum Physics, and UFOs (not to be confused with the other hiking trifecta: Sweat, Sunscreen, and Bug Repellant, which we had as well). For a few moments I left the eternally significant end of the pool and dove into the whimsically deep end.

This gave no rest from the questions posed by rock strata and the exposed cosmology in the desert. Instead, the discussion's intersection of God and Quantum Physics is an intellectual playground with tough questions and answers that vary from unverifiable to deeply disturbing. Why doesn't the Bible chronicle most of history? Where was my soul before I was here? Why can't science really explain the ends of "nothing"? I loved this conversation, there were many like it with Bradley, Ellie, and Zach.

It is important for me to discuss deep questions with the kids. Zach harbored a curious mind with a deep intellectual approach. He enjoys discussions and is energized when they transform into arguments. It's a blessing and a curse. He gets his approach from me and I got it from my dad. Arguing about who should mow the lawn is painful. Arguing about aliens is fun. Arguing about whether or not the moon is there when nobody is looking is pure-wilderness entertainment. It is why we leave the trail.

**Pure in Heart:** I find languages hard. I am not gifted in this area. I took German for three years in high school and struggled with it. Once, while working with the German

Air Force, I asked for some double-sided tape and got a tow truck. Spanish was no easier.

I worked through the computer software, started to read but could not understand when I listened. It was hard to speak to the men at the Mexican Restaurant because I could only understand ten to twenty percent of what they said. I couldn't figure out why they asked me if I wanted sand ("arena" in Spanish) with my meal but was pleased when they delivered a corn tortilla instead of flour ("harina", the 'h' is silent).

Satellite TV, something we brought into our house a year before so Ann could satiate her hunger for NASCAR races, now provided another cultural contribution. I watched Mexican TV. My ten to twenty percent comprehension was enough to understand that the news from Mexico communicated a very different worldview.

It struck me how so many people in Mexico lived lives of perpetual desperation. My poverty of wealth was oblivious to their needs but now this window into Mexico gave my heart a chance to peek through from time to time.

The hurricane that veered south, missing Texas and the Southern U.S. no longer seemed a 'near miss'. Instead this tempest was a direct hit on the people of the Yucatan. Was it really a blessing for our flock? Or a tragedy for other sheep? I felt a connection to those sheep.

As the week in the desert progressed Zach and I continued our adventures, our reading, our hot dinners in a cold desert, and our talks. We spent a night along the Escallante river and got lost returning to the truck. That "distinctive" rock formation next to our parked truck turned out to be one of many. Using only a compass we dead-reckoned across the desert for four miles. I missed the truck by a mile, luckily intersecting the faint remains of our road. We sat under a creosote bush and ate lunch. My fatherhood dead reckoning was much more accurate that week than my desert navigation.

The weather became increasingly cold throughout the week and we cancelled plans to hike down a flooded slot. Swimming in a dark hole at forty degrees lacked the fun-factor we looked for. We went down three other, less-committing slots, then into the Great Gallery. Here ancient petroglyphs grace the walls of Horseshoe (Barrier) Canyon.

The Great Gallery contains the most amazing ancient art in North America. The haunting figures, some as tall as nine-feet and are between 2,000 and 4,000 years old. A close look shows subtle details in the armless figures who seem to inhabit some world between ours and another. Until recently, this and two-dozen other pictograph sites were all that testified to these people. Zach and I stared at the art for hours then talked with two volunteer rangers who showed up long after we did.

We returned to the truck and drove home the next day. We had no answers from our trifecta discussion but being together in the desert made us more comfortable with the questions. On returning home I knew Zach and I were developing a relationship with significance. He made me a red shirt with "Plaid Canyoneering" on the front. I was proud to wear it and still do. The 2007 desert "dirt-bagging" trip will always be the week when Zach and I came together.

**Peacemakers:** The Agros project progressed almost on its own. Phil is a man of great passion, personal sacrifice, and possesses a love for all people. He needed a partner to organize the group. I volunteered to help him and we dove in. Soon a loose group of a dozen families came together committed to helping a yet undefined group of people in need. Our group was mostly from the company I worked at, peers who felt the need to contribute.

Agros employs a simple but innovative model. Started in 1982, Agros forms teams committed to a single group of people in one of four countries in Central America. Each group in the U.S. must commit to approximately half a million dollars over 5-8 years. It requires large groups of dedicated people. The money is used to develop a new village. The village typically consists of 30-40 families located in one of the countries. A plot of available land is identified and the families are loaned money to purchase this land. Advisers assist them in setting up a village government, agriculture, the infrastructure of life, and some additional income. If all goes right they pay back the loan in eight years and own their land.

I joined a "Journey With A Village". My life was intertwined with 33 families I'd never met thousands of miles away.

In April 2009 Zach, Ann, and I drove back to Southern Utah. This time we stayed in hotels and hiked during the days. Ann was more energetic for hiking than I had seen here since her hike to Camp Muir on Mt. Rainier six years before. She even hiked on her own when Zach and

I went biking. I hiked everyday that week, many early in the morning, by myself, seeking answers.

Unlike previous quests in the desert where the questions were around relationships with family, this one was about my middle fork. We started in Moab, Utah and progressed through the week to the Grand Canyon.

On our final full day I hiked to the Colorado River at Phantom Ranch for the second time. Fully prepared this time, I brought an entire bag of geology books in the car and carried a geology book and strata map with me in my pack. I read Genesis chapters one through three in Spanish before setting out at the trailhead. I was ready.

The top three thousand feet of strata passed before me as they had before. A short hike the previous day gave me the opportunity to preview these layers. I knew, now, they were the first few chapters of the book. The total strata were many tens of thousands of feet deep and lay across the entire Southwest, folded, tucked, and eroded.

Leaving the Tonto Plateau I finally saw the Grand Canyon Supergroup. It lay in full view for the next few hours as I crossed the river, had coffee at the Phantom Ranch Canteen, then hiked the connector trail from the South Kaibab to Bright Angel trail.

I had changed in the eight years since Bradley and I were here last. I do not claim to know the answers but am comfortable with the questions. There are no simple answers to the universe, the earth, or even how to spend the rest of my life.

**P**ersecuted for Righteousness: Stripped bare of its cloak of vegetation and top soil, the Southwest's geological strata literally screams their creator's name. Left to be discerned by those who could understand it, the layers tell a story which the book of Genesis does not. The limestones, shales, and sandstone reveal a God pre-scientific believers were incapable of facing. The scientific man, in his understanding, is overwhelmingly humbled.

The earth's geology is a revelation of God equal in insight and authority to that in the Bible. The study of God revealed through the Bible is theology. The study of God revealed through his creation is science.

*(Journal entry while in the Grand Canyon, 2009)*

The study of God revealed in each of us is simply love.

I returned from the desert physically tired, I walked 62 miles in five days yet was mentally and spiritually refreshed. As usually happens to me, solace for the soul does not reveal new intricacies but instead reinforces the obvious I already knew. God had a plan for me and I bought two tickets for Nicaragua, one for Ellie and one for me.

Ellie met us at home when we returned; obviously sad about the first 'family vacation' she could not go on. We went for a run. From behind our house we ran the usual two miles through the woods to the bridge across the Snoqualmie River. Instead of ritually tapping the concrete bridge pier and returning home, for the first time in fifteen years, we turned left and tried what I thought was a few hundred yards of old road along the riverbanks. Instead, we found miles of new trails, park, and forest.

The trail eventually turned up from the river and through a ravine. A small stream sang noisily as it cut among the thick trees. I was determined to find a way up out of the ravine and connect a loop to run back home. A "No Trespassing" sign preceded a barking, angry dog by about thirty feet so we eventually turned around. One more try up another trail dead-ended in someone's back yard.

I was frustrated at not finding the loop as we returned down the hill along the trail. Looking around, the trees were strangely different from the ones I was used to in this area near my house. One tree, next to the trail, was a full five feet in diameter. It turned out to be a snag, its top long broken off but another one up the hill was in excess of four feet. These were big trees for this logged out, farmed, and suburbanized area. I found a new, special forest within walking distance of home. It may simply be remarkable second growth, protected from a 30's-era fire that decimated this forest. It may be old growth. Either way, it was a pleasant reminder that serendipitous discoveries are not limited to the desert, they are everywhere around us.

That 2009 spring-break week in the desert with Zach and Ann was a time of contemplation and definition. I returned more at peace than I ever had been with my life, my destination, my mission, and God. It was all a bit over-wrought. Just as John Wesley Powell had been accused by one of his successors in the US Geological Survey, my thinking had "characteristically involved at the very least the universe, and generally the cosmos".

On the run back home, I noticed the first Trilliums blooming in between the ferns and rotting logs. Spring had reached the forest floor.

Few things in the Sand Shed film project would shape the documentary as much or affect me as deeply as the audio tapes of the old loggers. My interest in Middle Fork history started with the <u>Pratt River Logging Camp Evaluation</u> report eight months earlier and now that same report led me to the audio tapes.

The men who logged the Middle Fork and Pratt Valleys with the North Bend Timber Company were gone. Young in the 20's and 30's they passed away in the 80's and 90's. Providentially three were interviewed on tape for the logging camp evaluation. I contacted the Forest Service in early 2009 but little came of it. The cassette tapes were "in a box somewhere" with no known location. Late in May, I received an e-mail that the tapes were located, in a box in the Darrington Ranger Station. I couldn't convince the Forest Service's historian to let me borrow the tapes so I could listen to and digitally copy them but she would allow me to bring my equipment to the North Bend Ranger Station and copy these tapes. Ten hours of tapes. I took two days off work.

Sitting in the ranger station back office, the desk took on a certain mad-scientist look to it with my gear. An old-style tape player was connected to a very modern digital recorder through a series of four adapters. My laptop was positioned to take notes and an earphone cord drooped to the floor. Power cords tangled around my feet. I inserted the first cassette titled "Herb Ray tape 1".

# Chapter 10: Nueva Esperanza

The winter we stayed at the Pratt River. Now this is starting from the beginning. Now when we were just kids! I think when the Depression started there was nothing to do. Wasn't any jobs…no nothin' ya-know. So we went up there, trapping. I was trapping.

We stayed there in one of Mr. Vinnedge's cabins. He had two cabins there. Right about a mile below the mouth of the Pratt River. They called them the "Twin Cabins". Well we stayed in one of them. We got permission from Mr. Vinnedge you see……..So we went up there and were staying in his cabin. And I was catching a few muskrat and some mink and some skunks and a couple of bobcats.

Heh! The last wolves I ever saw was right up there! Because this Wilson of mine, he wasn't interested in trapping you know. I would go by myself, you know. I had one pair of snowshoes but I hardly ever used them after I got the trails broke down. And there was a big ole' place up there at the Halfway House. They called it the Halfway house just after you crossed Pratt River. That's the old Middle Fork Trail.

Well, I had traps set all around. We had quite a bit of snow. Probably, oh, 3-4 feet deep and it was well packed this time of year. I went up there one morning and I had to climb up out of the river bottom over kind of a bluff, you know. There was this big opening where the old Halfway house was and there had been quite a little of fresh snow and it had cleared off and the snow had a light crust on it.

Well I stuck my head up over that bank. I had a .22 Remington rifle with ten long-rifle shells in it, see. They're a pretty potent little weapon…22 with long rifles in 'em. And lo and behold I couldn't believe what I was lookin' at. Here was about half a dozen big black wolves out in this opening see…..”

*Herb Ray, logger in the Middle Fork
and Pratt Valleys during the 1930's,
in a 1989 taped interview.*

Ellie and I looked up into the crown of the big tree in front of us. The river sang its ever-present song behind as we explored this amazing forest garden growing deep in the valley. In the context of the past two years this was not a giant tree but it stood out in this forest not only due to its size but for the incredible diversity of other plants that grew in, on, and hung from it. I read a poem once that said in the jungle, there are "plants growing on plants growing on plants growing on trees". It was June 2009.

Our six-day trip was coming to an end and neither of us was ready to go home. Ellie and I started out in this deep, narrow, forested valley apprehensive and a little scared.

Birds sang almost constantly in the forest canopy and an occasional insect would buzz by but the unfamiliar terrain and startling challenges to many of our pre-conceived notions caused us to lay awake in the tent at night. Most insects were small here but occasionally a really large, interesting, and sometimes-beautiful bug landed for us to admire. It had been a long week but I was going to walk out, get in the mini-bus and cross the "Big River" with a completely different perspective. This time we were not in the Middle Fork Valley.

My "middle fork" brought me thousands of miles away to the mountains of Nicaragua. Ellie came with me to visit the people in a small village we were supporting in their efforts to purchase farmland and carve out a sustainable life. I came to Nueva Esperanza wondering what significance I would find in life with my kids leaving home and left understanding there were an additional 200 people in my family.

Ellie and I started the week with a flight to Managua, Nicaragua. Managua is a city beaten, scarred, and suffering. Its history has played out recently with a dictator, an earthquake, a hurricane, a civil war, and a multi-year battle with insurgents from a neighboring country bankrolled by a super power. Poverty was all around expressing itself in a myriad of ugly ways.

The Agros staff picked us up with the other five members of our service team at the Sandino Airport. Ellie and I flew in with Phil and his wife, Chris. We had problems in customs and I was pleased that I was able to work through them using my rudimentary Spanish. I was starting to find out why I was learning this beautiful language.

Pulling out of the airport we were immediately faced with people in great need. Kids washed our windows and expected money, vendors attempted to sell various small items, usually just as an excuse to ask for handouts. There was a portion of society here that was totally dependent on others with no hope to ever go beyond their disenfranchisement. I suspected Howard Thurman knew exactly where they were coming from and his writings helped me understand what I saw. The poor in Nicaragua, most of the population, desperately needs an alternative.

The next morning, after a good night's sleep in a local hotel, our driver stopped the little green mini-bus at the Oriental Market. Ostensibly looking for some sparklers for a planned event later in the week, we wandered through the stalls under strict control of the two Nicaraguan members of the Agros staff. A young boy came up and, using a local reed-like leaf, wove a small animal figure. He offered it to us as a "gift".

This was our first lesson on dependence, a trap and object lesson we fell right into. Being fundamentally suspicious, I would not let Ellie accept the "gift" even though the young boy insisted on it. Another member of the team took the little hand-made critter and placed it in her bag. A couple of minutes passed before the boy started asking for the money he expected for the little reed cricket. In no time, his kind, giving tone was gone and he was demanding compensation in a disrespectful and desperate extortion. A man, perhaps his father, materialized out of the crowd and backed him up. We quickly gave the little reed animal back, the boy left in a manner to gain sympathy, only to return later and attempt the same scam.

I felt for his situation but it was obvious the only person the little boy in the market respected less than us was himself. There were no easy answers for him or us. I was sure that giving him money for the little cricket would not help him and would only create more, unhealthy dependence. We continued through the market, returned to the mini-bus and drove out of Managua into the countryside.

Poverty was everywhere. I did not see a house that was even close to the worst house I knew of in my hometown of Redmond, Washington. Regularly there were small, crudely built huts and shelters, with a disheveled look. Yet there was an over-powering beauty everywhere with lush green plants, flowers, and towering volcanoes. Ellie and I watched out the window constantly, drinking in the newness of this strange and beautiful country.

Ellie commented on how nice the highway was. She was in Mexico City the weekend before helping with a summer camp and she said the roads were in much worse shape. That was her first time out of the country. It was a good preparation for this week and allowed her to learn some lessons in a practice situation before this much more involved trip.

Leaving Matagalpa, a mountain town of over 100,000 people, the road started to wind deeper into the terrain. The mountains were more rounded and smaller than Washington's. The road dove deeper and the pavement became rougher. The forest changed from sparse trees on pastoral expanses into a dense, multi-layered jungle. Exotic flowers, familiar to us only in stores, grew like weeds along the road. Birds of paradise, orchids, we stared in awe. I imagined scenes from the first <u>Indiana Jones</u> movie as we forded rivers and crossed narrow bridges missing slats and lacking any sort of guardrail.

El Tuma was the last town we passed through, a mountain outpost where we stopped to buy cheese. Horses were tied up across the street and an ox-drawn cart went by. People peered into the bus's windows at the obvious gringos. I felt exposed and nervous.

It took two hours driving on the twisted, rutted, and steep dirt road beyond El Tuma before we arrived at a group of isolated, non-descript houses. People stood next to a rutted path, at least 50 of them. They were short, the tallest woman perhaps 4'8" tall and the tallest man about 6 inches taller. They wore tattered, secondhand clothes with English writing none of them could probably read. Spying a small plywood sign nailed to a tree with "Nuevas Esperanzas" (we later found it was miss-spelled) with an arrow pointing to the right, I realized we were at our destination. We climbed out and looked across the track at the people we came to meet. Neither they nor we knew what to make of each other.

At least the men in the group knew what to do. They quickly gathered our bags on their backs and headed up the hill. Left standing at the intersection, we walked with the women and children, all of us strangers knowing only superficially our bond.

The four-wheel-drive track wound even more steeply up the hill and we could look out over the valleys and mountains of North-Central Nicaragua. Again, I couldn't get past how beautiful this was and how similar it was to the Middle Fork. One man, straggling behind the others, asked me what our trees and forests were like in the United States. We started to connect as we compared our jungle to theirs. I knew the Spanish words for "trees", "green", and "big". It was humid and I was sweating. Over the next six days I would get used to the heat and learn their names. His name is Benedicto.

Lying in bed the first night I stared at the tent ceiling. Tired, emotionally exhausted and wide-awake, I was trying to digest what I saw that day. The thirty-three families who lived in Nueva Esperanza had, a year earlier, been squatters on land 50-60 miles away. Along with another forty families who knew about Agros' work, they approached local representatives of the innovative organization from Seattle and asked to participate in their program to borrow money and acquire land. Two years of meetings to understand the commitment and high standards for responsibility and work resulted in fifty percent attrition.

The September before, while I scoured the Middle Fork for giant trees, they made a pilgrimage from the open rice and bean fields near Managua to this valley. Using money our group in Redmond had put together, they purchased land and started growing crops to feed themselves and sell to pay back their loan.

Agros had a manager to work with the people here. Ernesto was presented to us as an "agronomist" but he was much more. Trained as a medic and in agriculture, he taught, led, and coached them to become a village. Like Nicaragua as a whole, Ernesto's story is complex, painful, yet full of forgiveness, love, and Latin hospitality. He was a soldier for the Sandinista Army in the 1980's fighting the U.S. backed Contras. Grievously wounded in a battle where half his unit died, he recovered, went home, and started a new life. I was reluctant to tell him about my Air Force service during the 1980's.

The first task for the people in Nueva Esperanza was to clean up the area and prune the coffee plants. Next they moved quickly to plant food crops between the four-foot high coffee trees. Their progressive, diversified farming method was producing a rich set of crops, but they were far from ready. The bananas and malanga (a broad-leaf plant with an edible root-ball) was their current staple as they waited for their corn and beans to mature. Coffee was a cash crop, the way to pay back their land loan and move slowly out of poverty.

We visited each house, the seven of us with a translator meeting each family. We began to hear their stories. Phil, our leader, was a model of love, charity and listening. I had a hard time focusing, distracted by their sparse conditions and complete lack of possessions. Families of up to eleven lived in single ten by fifteen foot rooms. Their stone cocinas (stoves) sat in corners and poured smoke into their living areas. Signs of respiratory ailments were evident, an epidemic problem in rural Nicaragua. Some of the houses had 5-gallon plastic buckets with precious grain or beans. Many did not. Pots boiled on the cocinas, some with bananas, some with malanga, the wealthy few with beans.

In one house our interpreter, herself a native Nicaraguan who spent her teenage years in Florida, pointed out there was no smoke, no fire, the cocina was cold. "They will not eat today, there is no food". I started to choke up and had to look the other way. That moment haunted me as the week went on. I had never met someone without food.

Ellie clung to me throughout the first two days. Once I went to get the camera and when I got back she asked me to stick with her. She was in the same overwhelming adjustment period as me. On the first day a girl asked to have her earrings. We learned a few hours later she was from another village, the people of Nueva Esperanza realized the incursion of several children as we arrived, set up guards, and brought that activity to a halt. The people of Nueva Esperanza knew, as did we, that we couldn't give them anything because it would produce the very dependency and helplessness we all knew plagued the poor and that they were working to escape.

By the end of the second day we were getting to know our new friends. I found I could approach them at their houses and sustain a conversation in Spanish. Ellie started playing with the kids. We broke out some drawing pads and pencils for the kids and they drew until it was too dark to see. They returned the pencils, understanding the rules and even offered the papers back. We told them the drawings were theirs to keep.

Early the next morning I sat by the road sketching one of the thousands of beautiful plants when Menard, a young boy who was drawing the night before, walked by. I asked where he was going and he said "down the hill". There were houses there, the ones the mini-bus dropped us off by three days before. Some of those houses had special windows to sell basic supplies as little stores. I walked with him and asked why he was going.

Menard pulled a five Cordoba coin from his pocket, worth about 25 cents, and said he earned it working in the fields. He was going to one of the shops to buy a pencil. He wanted to draw. He never asked anyone to *give* him a pencil.

None of the three shops had a pencil to sell Menard that day. He said he would come back each day and eventually someone would have one. I realized then and there it was working. Menard's parents were teaching him you didn't ask others to give you something. Instead, you earned money and bought what you needed or wanted. It was the same tough love my parents gave me and I hurt with when I gave it to my kids. Menard knew he had some control over his circumstances and he was on his way to never being disenfranchised again.

That afternoon Ellie went with Ernesto and some of the local men on a delivery trip. Any time a vehicle goes anywhere in an area like rural Nicaragua there are a host of people who need rides and various items that need delivered. Ellie jumped in the back of the 4x4 Toyota pickup with three of the men and one other girl from our group and was gone for hours. Bouncing around the back roads of Matagalpa province they took people to town, delivered chilies to market, and got supplies for our meal the next day. It was the rainy season and one of Nicaragua's most remarkable downpours soaked Ellie and the rest of the crew in the back of the truck. Ellie came back invigorated; this was the place she had been looking for. Like me, Ellie was finding something very significant here. Something we both hoped for but dared not expect.

The week continued and we played baseball, sang songs, worked in the fields, picked, processed, and roasted some coffee, and generally just got to know each other. Sweat, dirt, mud, bug repellant, and sunscreen caked our clothing and us. Ernesto, with some help, built us a shower, a 55-gallon drum with a black-plastic screen, and cup for water. It was a nice gesture but most of us preferred to bathe in the river. Like the families living there, we went to the men's or women's areas, stripped down and bathed. The people of Nueva Esperanza made sure we had guards, always two people to ensure our safety. I was thankful for their care but frequently tested their ability to keep track of me. An ornery child in a jungle playground.

My Spanish was far from fluent but I could communicate. As the week went on the words began to flow and I asked questions. Only about ten percent of the families were rich enough to have chickens. Some owned as many as five but most only one or two. They ate the eggs, not the chickens. A nice lady named Aura Luz and two friends took two of us on a walk to visit the Evangelical and Catholic churches nearby. One was near the entrance, the other a "Latin 2 kilometers away". We talked most of the time. Aura was 30 years old and had three kids. She very much wanted a chicken so she could have eggs for herself and her children. "They are so rich" she said using a common Spanish description for food that is fulfillingly delicious. My heart bound into a knot and I turned to the depth of the jungle to hide my tears. I wished I could just give her a chicken.

We crossed a small river on our way back. Aura's two friends crossed right through in their sandal-clad feet. Aura offered to help us take off our shoes and cross the river but I bound across the dozen or so rocks spanning the thirty feet of shallow rapids. We all laughed at my dance. I was familiar with this kind of terrain.

Back at the village, hot and tired, we waited for the Toyota truck to return so we could all tell stories and sing. Ellie, Ernesto, and the rest were four hours late. Everyone simply got together for our gathering, dinner was hours late and no one seemed to care. The contrast with the "American way" was striking.

Ellie was excited about her bumpy, wet day and bonded with the men she road with. It was a turning point for Ellie individually and for our relationship with the people in Nueva Esperanza.

Each evening the seven of us from Redmond would gather to discuss the day and come to terms with our emotions. That evening we talked about what would happen with the kids in the village as they grow and start families of their own. Agros does not allow the purchase of additional property to add to the village so we assumed the kids would have to move away. It is a very American thing for our kids to move away as they come of age, not having enough house or possessions to provide for multiple families.

Lying in bed, I realized this was a U.S. paradigm. Nueva Esperanza would produce more and more food on the same land as their farming improved. More people could be supported at a reasonable living standard. A family can either split its wealth amongst the children or send them away to earn more. In the West, we choose to send our children off instead of dividing our wealth and multiplying our community. Thinking back on the days before when we visited each of the families, I realized a "family" could mean many people and multiple generations. There was so much to learn here in this warm land.

I visited a few of the families and asked about their new homes. Arnulfo Orosco Hernandez went with me up the hill and we walked his land. His house was just a frame, the walls not yet complete. He showed me where his flower garden would go and his new kitchen. The cocina was outdoors and would have a flue to carry the smoke away. His kids would be healthier. Ishmael Lopez Gonzales showed me his fields. He asked me to take his picture in front of his steep acre of land covered with five-foot tall corn plants. No US farmer would ever attempt to grow corn on that near-cliff. I asked Santos Dormus Hernandez about his new house. He said we were sleeping in it. I tried to imagine letting someone else sleep in my new home before I did. This was only one example of their generosity.

One day rolled into another. We worked, we talked, we played baseball, we sang songs. Ellie and I did not want to leave and the people there didn't want us to go. On the last full day I asked the thirty three men to sign my Spanish Bible. Jose David Dormus was only 17 and cared for his brothers, sisters, mother, and grandparents. His father ran away and left them, a boy stepped up and proved he was a man.

There were many tears. One man said "this is the happiest week of my life", he never dreamed he would have such a wonderful time. I prayed it would not be the best week of his life in a few years. Aura Luz cried and cried. She would miss us and we would miss her. They knew what we did for them but were surprised by the people behind the money and loan. We now knew what they did for us and were surprised with the bond we now had.

On the drive back we dropped one of the families off in Managua and then proceeded to Granada, Nicaragua's tourist town. Ellie and I were regretting scheduling an extra day for sightseeing; we just wanted to fly home. Arriving at our hotel in Granada, we cleaned up completely for the first time in the week and took a walk. We talked about what happened and started to come to terms with what it meant to each of us.

Ellie said, "I feel so sorry for those girls, the ones who were only 17 and were already married and had kids." I replied they were probably saying how they felt so sorry for Ellie, here she was 19 and still didn't have a husband. We laughed and recognized how much we learned about seeing the world through their eyes. We realized how much more there is to learn.

Ellie wants to come back and spend more time. She started listing her plans to meet with the Agros people in Seattle, learn more about the opportunities, and plan how she could help. She felt a purpose she had never felt before this trip.

I was equally convicted. I saw an opportunity for a purpose beyond raising my three kids. I saw the opportunity to take on a whole new phase in life. There was much to do and much to learn. I wanted even more to be able to actually converse in Spanish. I need to work hard to focus how I spend money in order to have the funds to come back here, and I would have to prioritize my vacation time. There was no question in my mind, this was my direction.

For the first time in many years I felt a real significance. I was not just accepting my purpose on faith, I could feel the significance of that purpose. I read the Bible in Spanish and the words came alive. I could understand far more than I did at the beginning of the week. There was a new definition and fewer questions in my life.

Ellie and I walked around Granada and began to understand the Nicaragua outside of Nueva Esperanza. We went to the local market, mingled in the square, and looked into the volcano. It occurred to me I just might have found my sheep. For the first time in 21 years I felt that same wave of emotion I first felt on the Loring Air Force Base flightline after launching the medivac flight to help save an unborn baby's life.

I fully realized the implications of that forested valley deep in the mountains northeast of Matagalpa. I have family in Nicaragua. I have a "New Hope"*.

*Nueva Esperanza is Spanish for "New Hope"

# Chapter 11: Turning Left

The big trees were in the Middle Fork long before the North Bend Timber Company loggers came to cut down their neighbors, long before the miners, the hot springs bathers, the hikers, the tree hunters, and the documentary film makers. The big trees are a subtle reminder of what is timeless and what is not. Contemplating their place in history puts ours in perspective.

I needed to work on the film project with Zach but life was not so simple to let me focus on historical photographs and taped interviews with loggers.

Two years prior I told my sister's husband I would help him climb Rainier if he ever wanted to. The commitment demanded little over the next two years with Will working long hours, traveling, and upgrading the house he and my sister bought. Ellie's, Bradley's, and my glowing stories about climbing in August 2008 changed that. He approached me and asked if we could climb together in 2009.

Will and I trained together all winter. Hiking, practicing technical skills like knots, and ice travel. I enjoyed being with him and the training came easy. Ellie joined us and indicated she wanted to climb too. The three of us decided to climb earlier in the year than usual, in spring instead of August.

By May I was pre-occupied and didn't really want to give up a weekend. The winter was harder than we were used to, although less than the old loggers spoke of, so the Mountain was still in winter condition in Mid-May. Finally, the last two weeks brought warm weather, the snow settled, and the last weekend in May looked good.

I called Bradley; he planned to climb that weekend with some friends. They bagged out on him. I was excited to hear he could climb with us. He called back the next day and the news wasn't good. The Army wouldn't let him go, they wanted to make sure he was in good shape for his primary ROTC training in June. They felt climbing presented too large a risk for injury. The Army had my best man.

For the first time in nine years I roped up for a major climb without Bradley. For the first time in three years I tied into the lead position on the rope.

Nine hours into climbing the upper mountain I heard the terrified scream "Falling!" It came from Ellie. I went down hard, dug my ice axe into the Styrofoam-like ice and looked down the rope. Our "fourth", a friend who trained with me before but couldn't climb in 2008, looked at me. I screamed at him to "dig in!"

Silence. Ellie and Will were over a small rise in the glacier so I couldn't see them. There was an eerie silence.

Then I heard Ellie. She was ok and didn't fall. She yelled back saying Will fell, slid down the ice and was hanging there from the rope. I realized Ellie was in control of the situation and her quick reaction arrested Will's slide towards a cavernous crevasse opening.

Ellie, no longer new to this game, was now a climber. She summitted The Mountain for her third time and we danced on the summit. I stared at her in disbelief, so much had changed.

I missed Bradley.

A great story sets a scene, develops characters, reveals a drama, endures a challenge, and ends in a triumph. When I started this story I was sure of my triumph. I confidently began writing despite most of the lines not yet lived yet solidly anticipated. I firmly believed this was a story of giant trees and completing a successful quest.

I was firmly convinced I would find a tree of distinction in the Middle Fork Valley. Each night I envisioned myself being recognized as the guy who found "the big tree". It never occurred to me that, in the end, the story wouldn't even be about trees.

For me, there has been no mid-life crisis. The decisions, questions, and changes I face are not unique to my forties. They are the important aspects of life's continuous transformation.

I think the world puts too much emphasis on this forty-something crisis. We search for a set of answers that will lead to happiness in the second halves of our lives yet miss happiness when it develops in the same way it did in the first half of our life. Happiness springs up when we introspectively recognize the need to change and grow then follow through on the actions necessary to attain that growth.

I wonder how many marriages are permanently scarred by this tragic rush to solve all of life's problems in some sort of mid-life change. How many people leave the love of their life, maybe the only real partner who can ever stand them, because they believe there is a simple answer? The illusion of simple answers supplants the reality of constant self-assessment and renewal.

Looking forward, I see that Ann and I have our own transformation to go through. I love her very much, much more than when I met her twenty-seven years ago. I am always amazed at the number of men who carry old pictures of their wives taken ten, twenty, fifty years ago. When asked why, their response is "she hasn't changed". I realize now, after being married almost twenty-five years, why. Ann hasn't changed. That beautiful girl who I fell in love with is still who I see. That is Ann.

But our lives have changed. The kids are moving away so, after twenty-one consecutive years of centering ourselves on our kids, we look across the dining room table and try to figure out who is sitting on the other side. It triggers a deep fear. That fear, that urge to run blindly down Nason Ridge, that trepidation the night before a big climb, that gnawing rot in the stomach as rocks clatter down a hillside, is here now as I look forward to where Ann and I will go.

I have friends who left their wives at about the same stage in life I am at now. I can't completely get inside their heads but somehow every player in their story changed so much they agreed they weren't right for each other anymore. I do not want that to happen but, as this is written, I can't guarantee where Ann and I are going.

I am comforted in the lessons I learned over the past couple of years. Developing a new relationship with Ann is simply the subject of the next transformation in my life. It is not about simple answers or a single thing that needs changed. We have to transform and it will take years to do so. It could be a crisis but it is not "the crisis". Instead, it is one of life's many tough challenges and demands we work through it.

I harbor a grand desire to develop the relationship with Ann worthy of my deep love for her. I am confident that I will not run down the ridge, blindly. I developed the ability to take on the darkness and confidently press forward when the voice says it will all be ok. He will take care of it. I can already see that our newly found family in Nicaragua is changing Ann too.

For Christmas, Ann gave me a new wedding ring. My old one was small and worn, a reminder of how little we had when we married in 1985. Although I selected the ring, I was surprised when I opened the box to find "forever" engraved inside. It felt good to know Ann and I shared confidence in our future.

There are really two types of great stories, heroic tales and tragedies. I hoped for a heroic tale. I am pleased this is not a tragedy. I am more positive than ever that I would prefer to live a life in between. Even in the heroic tales, the hero is frequently a tragic figure.

A life well lived is incredibly simple and equally ubiquitous. It is enjoying all of the characters I am surrounded by. It is learning from the few great figures in life. It is influencing a few others. It is accepting that I do not get to know all of the answers. More than anything, it is accepting what God gives as it comes, day by day. It is the journey, not the destination.

In spite of my expectations for a heroic tale or tragedy, the story finds significance in the journey. I think Oliver Wakelam and Bill Longwell would have appreciated this. Their lives exemplified this, they were significant because of how they lived not for what they accomplished.

I spent the first forty years of my life believing there were mountaintops for me to obtain. A great destiny. A lofty view where I can see many days into my future. Vast horizons for me.

I found instead, God made me for the valleys. Deep in the forest, accepting each day's journey will take me across a dozen new and unexpected horizons. The ultimate paradox is, like this story, the harder I plan the future the less likely it is to follow my plan.

There are no simple answers. I like that. It is what I learned during the middle fork of my life.

I think if I found the largest tree in Washington, I would have named it the Oliver Wakelam tree. A minor gesture that is completely unnecessary. Oliver's honor lies not in some monument but in the heritage he created. Bradley, Ellie, and Zach each carry his heritage in their hearts. Bradley Oliver Allen also carries it in his name.

There are few truly great people yet we all have the opportunity to be great from time to time. Significance comes from great works performed by average men. That is the way I turned during this middle fork.

Hand over the lead. Help the poor. Build a fire. Film a movie.

Be a dad.

Zach and I practiced shooting for our movie on the spindly Douglas fir down the road from our house. Garbage cans lined the unkept street below as we argued over why we were doing this.

"We are doing this to practice" I replied with no effort to hide the annoyance I felt inside. Zach was obviously ready to film and be done.

The creation of project Sand Shed got off to a very rough start. Zach's and my fierce independence, wanton creativity, and painful similarities were driving each other nuts. Just discussing the film script turned into sharp words, crass snipes, and an argued end to the discussion.

Not the best venue for Zach and me, these collaborative sessions broke down quickly and we ended up watching TV in silence. Only our favorite sitcom about a bunch of brainy science geeks could get us out of our collaborative funk. If the idea of Sand Shed was to cement a life-long bond between Zach and I, it wasn't working.

But the film continued to come together as the spring of 2009 warmed and rained into summer. Although at first frustrated by the washed-out Middle Fork Road and our inability to access our film sites, it actually worked well for Zach and me, giving us time to research the story, develop the script, and figure our gear out. We may have been in the worst recession in seventy years but I was a one-man stimulus package, buying a new computer, editing software, High Definition digital video camera, and host of sound equipment.

A visit to a friend who did filmmaking professionally helped a lot and his comments on scripts gave both Zach and me some ideas on how to lay out our plot. I used a template

Zach brought home from school and created a visual format that allowed me to sit and write the script then give it to him. He reviewed the script, made comments, and we took it out to our film location. The little Douglas fir by the garbage cans was a poor substitute for an old growth giant but the experience showed us how to work together.

In the first test of our new collaborative method, we went to North Bend and filmed some driving sequences. Using our two-column graphic script, the filming moved from site to site with ease. It wasn't perfect, we had to go back the next week for some second takes but Zach and I began to be a team.

The real test came in July when Zach, my friend Dave, and I waded through the Middle Fork River and bushwhacked our way into the Pratt Valley carrying packs overloaded with film gear. Starting at the Sand Shed site, where not much remained of the little shack for drying sand, we filmed forest, artifacts and hiking sequences. Using GPS coordinates recorded during three previous excursions into the Pratt, we went right to the sights we needed with little or no searching.

Dave built a clever device that we strung between trees and pulled our video camera along on a carriage. The camera's motion, far different than might be seen with a tripod, started to give our project a professional feel. It was a long day; twelve hours, three river crossings, seven miles of hiking, numerous bug bites, and at least a mile of pushing through sticker-bushes, but definitely worth it. Zach worked all day as the director of film, worked the camera, and directed the shots.

We especially enjoyed shooting the scene of the post holders on the two over-turned flatbed cars partially buried along the Pratt railroad grade. They were the spark for our creative fire the previous year and were why we were there. It is probably not a coincidence that these two rotting log-cars sit in the exact area Dick Kirby saw a rail car thirty years before. Another loose end fell into place.

Our final film shot for the day was at the Big Trees sign. I set up the tripod, carefully leveled it, and Zach mounted the camera. Zach cleaned the lens, checked the camera settings, and adjusted the white balance. We needed hikers so Dave and I performed as actors.

Dave and I walked up the trail and past the Big Trees sign. "Big Trees" to the right. "Trail" to the left. Without even slowing down, we symbolically turned left and went up the valley to our little part of Middle Fork history.

I feel great about Project Sand Shed, video, history, big tree art, and the bond with my son Zach.

I haven't stopped looking for big trees.

# Oatmeal Travel Bars

Originally developed for climbing, these work extremely well as airplane food.

<u>Ingredients</u>:

½ Cup melted Margarine

1 Cup whole-wheat flour

½ Cup brown sugar

½ Cup white sugar***

½ tsp baking powder

½ tsp baking soda

1 egg

¼ Cup milk***

1 tsp vanilla

3 ½ Cups Oatmeal (regular, not quick)

<u>Flavoring (use one)</u>:

- ½ cup raisins, 1 cup Craisins, 1 tsp cinnamon (w/ cinnamon sprinkled on top)

- 1 cup raisins and 1 tsp cinnamon (plus cinnamon sprinkled on top)

- ½ cup craisins, ½ cup shredded coconut

- 1 tsp maple flavoring, 1 cup chopped walnut

## Method:

Pre-heat oven to 350°

Melt margarine

Mix dry ingredients (except for oatmeal) in large bowl

Add wet ingredients, mix well

Add melted margarine, mix well

Add oatmeal, mix well

Add flavoring

Let stand 5 minutes

Pour into greased 9" baking dish

Bake 15 minutes at 350°, remove from oven and pre-cut into 15 bars, bake for another 10 minutes at 350°.

Makes 15 bars (total: 2,500 calories/65 g fat, fifteen bars gives 175 calories/4.5 g fat each). Will keep 3-5 days wrapped in plastic wrap or 4-6 months if frozen.

***OK to substitute ½ cup honey for white sugar. If you do this, do not add milk

# My List of Great Men I Know

Don Allen (the greatest)

Bruce Taber (the friend who can keep up)

Colonel Bob Reynolds (the leader)

Lt. Colonel William Northcutt (he gave all)

Ward Bushnell (the boss I miss)

Dave Hunt (my wisest friend)

Don Sytsma (doing business as Christ would)

Chris Matson (taught me not to be a jerk)

Bradley Allen (the lead dog)

Zach Allen (red rock partner)

Reverend Paul Johnson (what you believe matters)

Reverend Fred Davis (he cared for us)

Reverend Ed Randal (loves all)

Bill Longwell (taught me to hike)

Ray Rister (taught me to build a house)

Oliver Wakelam (a hard life, lived well)

# Bibliography

A Cultural Resource Overview: Prehistory, Ethnography, and History Mt. Baker-Snoqualmie National Forest by Jan Hollenbeck, United States Forest Service, Aug 1987.

Beyond the Hundredth Meridian: John Wesley Powell and the Second Opening of the West, Wallace Stegner, Penguin Books, 1992.

The Challenge of Rainier by Dee Molenaar, The Mountaineers, 1971.

Eiger Dreams, by John Krakauer, Anchor Books, Doubleday, 1990.

A Field Guide to Mammal Tracking in North America by James Halfpenny, Johnson Books., 1986.

Forest Giants of the Pacific Coast by Robert Van Pelt published by the Global Forest Society, 2001.

Into the Wild, John Krakauer, Anchor Books, 1997.

Jesus and the Disinherited, Howard Thurman, Beacon Press Books, 1976.

Kinsey Photographer: The Locomotive Portraits by Dave Bohn and Rodolfo Petschek, Black Dog and Leventhal Publishers, Inc. 1984.

101 Hikes in the Alpine Lakes by Harvey Manning

<u>Pratt River Logging Camp Evaluation</u> an archeological report prepared for the Mt. Baker-Snoqualmie National Forest by S.A. Boswell, S.K. Campbell, L.C. McConaghy, and C.J. Miss, Northwest Archeological Associates, Inc., December 19, 1990.

<u>Rober Vinnedge's private letters</u>, provided for review by Gardiner Vinnedge of North Bend, WA., circa 1920-1940.

<u>Shay Catalog</u> reprinted in 1979 by Pacific Fast Mail, Edmonds, Washington.

<u>Taped interviews with Loggers from the NBTC,</u> provided by the US Forest Service, 1989, tapes held in USFS archives.

<u>Walking with The Poor: Principles and Practices of Transformational Development</u>, by Bryant L. Myers, World Vision, 2004.

<u>Wild at Heart</u>, by John Elderedge, Nelson Books, 2001.

<u>Wild Trees</u> by Richard Preston, Random House, 2007.

<u>Wood & Iverson: Loggers of Tiger Mountain</u> by Ken Schmelzer Oso Publishing, 2001.

NOTE: This page is intentionally left blank. Feel free to use it to start a fire if your feet are cold. If you are like my dad, it will only take this one sheet to start your fire. If you are like me, feel free to order a new book on your return home.